From The Publisher's Pen

Hello, and welcome to the new, re-vamped Autograph Quarterly. We are glad to have you aboard!

For the last two years a collector by the name of Samuel Xidas from London started and published six issues of Autograph Quarterly. While I never wrote for the magazine I did help him gain advertisers, subscribers, and the like. He is still a strong collector now in his 70s (sorry Sam), but across the pond and financing it all himself, he felt he couldn't stay on track with the magazine, and the field has had enough of those, so he graciously allowed me to buy the magazine.

Magazines are said to be going the way of the dinosaur, and that may be but as a dealer for over thirty years now, I remember how much I liked reading autograph magazines and now, while our hobby is arguably larger than ever before, there are none. Sure, the clubs issue periodic magazines. Both the Manuscript Society and UACC do, but there are no paid subscription, mainstream magazines and as a past writer for Autograph Collector, as well as a regular columnist and contributing editor, I know a little bit about what was popular and what wasn't, and what fans and collectors asked for the most in those pages.

So, with the help of two wonderful investors, here we are – launching the only in-print magazine in the field, and yes, you can buy this magazine as a Kindle on amazon.com and yes, you can buy it and download it directly off of the new website at autographquarterly.com.

So let me tell you a little of my vision. Unlike many newbie collectors, I know that eBay isn't the end all, be all of knowledge in our marketplace. In fact, it's a terrible place to sell unless you are selling a truly one of a kind item. Even then, it is entirely predicated, like all auctions, on who is bidding when it ends, period. That winner could be a dealer re-selling the piece later. So eBay auctions are and have always been a terrible place to try and watch price trends, hence the fact that we are brining into these pages a "What's Hot and What's Not" feature and a Price Guide update as well.

Runners: those triumphant autograph seekers who stand out in the elements for days on end to secure the tougher autographs in the field will have a voice. Finally, for the first time anywhere, they will have their own column and tell tips and their own stories. (Send those stories in runners!)

With News from Abroad, you can see the autograph trends in other countries. With the Autograph Bookshelf, we will review any and all submissions. No politics here!

In fact, that's a promise I'm going to make right here, right now. This isn't a bully pulpit and never will be. This isn't a magazine to promote my company, or a magazine to promote my ideas or ideals in the field. Is the field in trouble? Most assuredly and most seasoned dealers know who and what is hurting us, so going over that in any magazine or website is foolish and non-productive. What I will be doing is bringing in the timeliest news, greatest writers in the field, and cover in each issue every part of autograph collecting.

I want you collecting one other thing; these issues, so get your subscription in now. There are several key freebies that more than pay for it in each issue which only subscribers will get. Look in the pages and you will see what you missed if you picked this up on the newsstand, and yes, we will have newsstand coverage. We will be appearing at a dozen or more trade shows per year. Come by our booth at The Hollywood Show and say hello for one, and our investors are going to do what they do best: spend money! Starting with this issue, several thousand copies are being printed and mailed free to every known collector we can find. We want them to get a taste. We're sure that you will come back for more. A magazine by collectors for collectors - isn't that what the hobby needs? To put the fun back into collecting and help learn about our wonderful hobby along the way?

One naysayer said there would be a conflict of interest with a dealer owning the magazine. Guess what? A dealer has owned every magazine that was ever

in print in this field, so there's nothing new there. Wouldn't you rather someone with experience in the field own it? I will let the content speak for me on that score.

Finally, I want to thank all of the great submissions in this issue. From the groundbreaking Andy Griffith article that should stop some of the secretarials always seen on eBay to Seth Kaller's article on the origins of The Night Before Christmas, and Tracks joining us from abroad, I thank each and every one of you for showing you care about the hobby and are not just in it for a buck. Thank you all!

Until the next issue – Happy Collecting!

Kevin Martin

Steve McQueen
$695.00

Marlon Brando
$695.00

Marilyn Monroe
$2,495.00

Walt Disney - $1,495.00
Marlene Dietrich - $195.00
"Houdini" - $795.00
Douglas Fairbanks, Sr. - $250.00
Cecil B. DeMille - $350.00
Mother Teresa - $425.00
Henry Fonda - $250.00
Jimi Hendrix - $1,495.00
George Burns - $125.00
George Reeves - $695.00
Colin Clive - $595.00
Liberace (with Piano Drawing) - $295.00
Buddy Holly - $795.00
Lupe Velez – $225.00
Margaret Hamilton - $250.00
"Dr. Seuss" (Theodor Seuss Geisel) - $395.00
Rocky Marciano - $450.00
Marilyn Monroe - $2,495.00
Frank Lloyd Wright - $595.00
"Laurel & Hardy" - $895.00
Helen Hayes - $125.00
Michael Jackson - $325.00
Lon Chaney, Sr. - $795.00
Clark Gable & Vivien Leigh - $595.00
Amelia Earhart - $625.00
Ernest Hemingway - $3,150.00
Edward G. Robinson - $250.00
Carole Lombard - $275.00
"The Blues Brothers" - $495.00
Grace Kelly - $395.00
"The Apollo XI Crew" - $6,595.00
U.S. Grant - $595.00
Basil Rathbone - $295.00
Mary Astor - $250.00
Geronimo - $8,595.00
Gary Cooper - $250.00
Cary Grant - $295.00
Casey Stengel - $495.00
W. C. Fields - $395.00
Jimmy Stewart & Donna Reed - $325.00
Jimmy Stewart - $125.00
Jimmy Stewart & June Allyson - $195.00
Jimmy Stewart & Maureen O'Hara - $195.00
Jimmy Stewart & Frank Capra - $295.00
Jimmy Stewart & Marlene Dietrich - $350.00

James Dean - $2,295.00
"The Maltese Falcon" - $2,195.00
Steve McQueen - $695.00
Sigmund Freud - $1,295.00
Martin Luther King, Jr. - $2,495.00
"The Wizard of Oz" - $2,195.00
Oscar Wilde - $1295.00
Judy Garland - $395.00
Frederic Remington - $525.00
Charles M. Russell - $495.00
James Dean & Sal Mineo (on same page) - $2,995.00
Natalie Wood - $295.00
Frank Sinatra - $395.00
Gerald R. Ford - $295.00
Maxfield Parish - $295.00
Alberto Vargas - $425.00
Salvador Dali - $395.00
Erte - $250.00
Marc Chagall - $450.00
Andy Warhol - $425.00
Katharine Hepburn - $275.00
Alfred Hitchcock - $895.00
Rita Hayworth - $295.00
Edgar Allan Poe - $7,995.00
Harold Lloyd - $325.00
Will Rogers - $595.00
Wiley Post - $250.00
Lech Walesa - $295.00
Mary Pickford - $225.00
Charles A. Comiskey - $650.00
John, Lionel & Ethel Barrymore - $595.00
John Phillip Sousa - $395.00
Samuel Goldwyn - $225.00
Louis B. Mayer - $250.00
Eddie "Rochester" Anderson - $195.00
Kurt Vonnegut - $150.00
Marilyn Monroe & Joe DiMaggio - $2,995.00
Claudette Colbert - $150.00
"The DiMaggio Brothers" - $1,295.00
Clayton Moore - $125.00
Eubie Blake - $150.00
Joe DiMaggio (Signed Baseball) - $695.00
Ted Williams (Signed Baseball) - $595.00
Mickey Mantle (Signed Baseball) - $695.00

Mark Twain - $1,195.00
Walter Huston - $175.00
Ty Cobb - $795.00
Charles Laughton - $195.00
Hal Roach - $195.00
"Gilligan's Island" Cast Photo (All 7) - $695.00
Spencer Tracy - $275.00
Jim Morrison - $895.00
Jerry Garcia - $395.00
Ronald Reagan - $395.00
Connie Mack - $695.00
Duke Ellington - $295.00
James Cagney - $175.00
James Cagney & Corinne Calvet - $225.00
Bud Abbott & Lou Costello - $695.00
Tallulah Bankhead - $175.00
Brigitte Bardot - $125.00
Enrico Caruso - $325.00
Lillian Gish - $125.00
Alger Hiss - $295.00
Bela Lugosi - $695.00
Truman Capote - $225.00
"The Marx Brothers " - $1,395.00
Fay Wray - $175.00
"The Three Stooges" Moe, Curley (first names), Larry (full name) - $1,495.00
Lucille Ball & Desi Arnaz (Full Names) - $595.00
Menachem Begin - $395.00
Yul Brynner – $195.00
Shirley Temple - $295.00
Marlon Brando - $695.00
Madonna (nude) - $275.00
Margaret Thatcher - $295.00
Peter Lorre - $275.00
Muhammad Ali - $225.00
Roland Winters "Charlie Chan" - $125.00
Fred Astaire & Ginger Rogers - $395.00
Ronald Colman - $175.00
Eric Clapton - $75.00
Linus Pauling - $175.00
Humphrey Bogart - $695.00
Boris Karloff - $2,250.00
"Father Knows Best" Cast Photo (all 5) - $495.00
Buck Jones - $295.00
John F. Kennedy - $1,895.00

Walt Disney
$1,495.00

Frank Sinatra
$395.00

'Houdini'
$795.00

Marilyn Monroe & Joe DiMaggio
$2,995.00

'The Maltese Falcon'
$2,195.00

"The DiMaggio Brothers"
Vince, Joe and Dom • $1,295.00

Lucille Ball & Desi Arnaz $595.00

Lon Chaney Sr.
$795.00

Autograph Quarterly
Created by Collectors for Collectors

Published by Kevin Martin
www.autographquarterly.com / www.pieceofthepast.com

Contributing Writers:
Tracks U.K. – www.tracks.co.uk
Seth Kaller – www.sethkaller.com
Nelson Deedle – www.iconographs.com
Philip Marsh – philipmarsh@aol.com
Larry Rafferty – www.MrBebop.com
Dorina Marian
Stephen Koschal – www.stephenkoschal.com
Todd Mueller – www.toddmuellerautographs.com

Article and Book Review Submissions should be sent to
Autograph Quarterly Magazine
1240 East Ontario Avenue, Suite 102-307
Corona, CA 92881

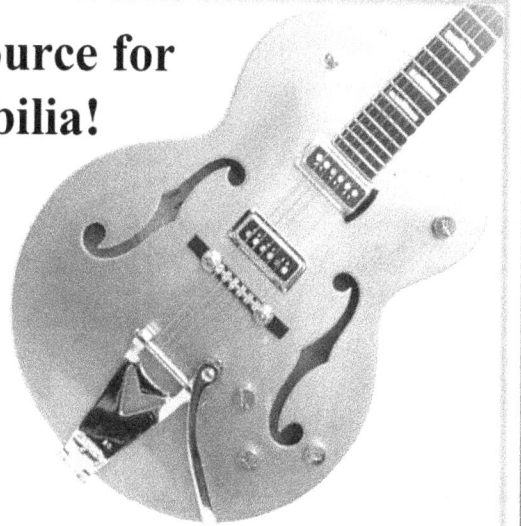

"The White Album Auction"

TracksAuction.com

- The first fully signed 'White Album' ever to be auctioned.

- Expected to realize over $100k at auction

- Taken in lieu of a $100 debt in the '70s by a London man

The Beatles – An American 1968 stereo pressing of 'The Beatles' LP commonly referred to as 'The White Album', autographed by all four Beatles on the inner gatefold. This is the rarest fully signed Beatles album ever to be publicly auctioned. The autographs are undoubtedly one of the finest sets ever to appear on a signed Beatles album. The formation of each signature is virtually perfect, they are extremely fluid, bold and vivid. It is a large, attractively spaced set of signatures. John Lennon and Paul McCartney have signed in black pen with John adding self portraits of himself and Yoko Ono, he has also dated his autograph "Dec 73". George Harrison and Ringo Starr have signed in blue pen. Paul, George, and Ringo have not dated their autographs but we have inspected them closely comparing them to other authentic signatures in our reference files from 1973/74 and found them to be perfectly typical examples from this period.

John Lennon's autograph was most probably signed in the U.S.A., after John left England on August 31, 1971. He never returned to the U.K. We do not know whether the autographs of Paul, George and Ringo were signed in the U.K. and then the album was taken to the U.S.A. by an Apple employee, for example, where it was signed by John, or vice versa. The possibility that Paul, George and Ringo also signed in the U.S.A. is more remote as Paul could not enter the U.S.A. because of his drug related convictions before he was issued a visa in December 1973. His first visit was in March, 1974. We believe that the first occasions in 1974 that Ringo and George were in the States were February and October, respectively.

This highly attractive set of autographs was signed on what many consider to be The Beatles' greatest work. Recording began on May 30, 1968 and finished on October 17th later that year. It consumed more studio hours than any other Beatles LP. Derek Taylor, the group's press officer, writing at the time of the LP's release, saw the White Album as evidence of the fact that "Lennon and McCartney are the greatest songwriters since Schubert." The album is an eclectic mix of styles and tunes which swoops and soars to heights unprecedented even by The Beatles' exceptionally high standards. *Back in the U.S.S.R., While My Guitar Gently Weeps, Happiness is a Warm Gun, I'm So Tired, Yer Blues, Helter Skelter, Why Don't We Do It in the Road* – recordings of sublime quality that would stand out in any musical era or within any genre of music. John Lennon had particularly fond memories of his input into the album. In his Rolling Stone interview he commented, "I keep saying that I always

preferred the double album, because my music is better on the double album. I'm being myself on it."

The album also arguably contained George Harrison's and Ringo Starr's finest moments. Paul McCartney in an interview recorded for *The Beatles Anthology* video series made a remark that was both designed to brush aside any criticism of the LP and at the same time, draw attention to the magnitude of the work. With a magnanimous wave of his hands, he humorously snapped, "Shut up will ya? It's *The Beatles White Album!*"

Autographed Beatles albums are amongst the rarest types of Beatles items. During 1962/63, the period in which The Beatles signed most frequently in order to please their fans, the most usual surface upon which the group's signatures were obtained was on a page in an autograph book. Beatles LPs and photos, etc. were more unwieldy and less easy to carry to concerts. Hence, few were autographed. The most commonly signed album was the U.K. *Please Please Me* album, followed by the group's second U.K. album, *With The Beatles*. Following these two 1963 releases, autographed Beatles albums become increasingly scarce as John, Paul, George, and Ringo generally became less interested in signing autographs. Mid-period albums such as Beatles for Sale, Help! and Rubber Soul are very rarely seen autographed by the group. During 1967, the group shunned the limelight and esconced themselves in the recording studio. They were seldom contactable for signatures except by the girls waiting outside EMI's Abbey Road studios. Only a handful of *Sgt. Pepper* LPs were autographed. Signed Beatles albums from "The Studio Years" are becoming increasingly desirable because they are increasing in value faster than any other type of collectively signed Beatles item. An attractively signed copy of *Sgt. Pepper* recently reached $290,500.00 in a U.S. auction, double its prevailing retail value.

However, it is the late period Beatles albums – *The White Album, Abbey Road,* and *Let It Be* – which are the scarcest of all signed Beatles albums. (Incidentally, American albums autographed by the group are far rarer than their English counterparts. Only around 12 signed U.S.A. LPs bearing the autographs of John, Paul, George and Ringo are known to exist.) Until we came across this signed copy of *The White Album* (which has nestled in the storage cabinet of a sixties radiogram in South London for the last 40 plus years, totally unbeknown to the owner that the signatures were genuine!) we had never seen, anywhere in the public domain, a genuine autographed example of this LP in our 24 years of trading in Beatles autographs.

The World Famous *Abbey Road*

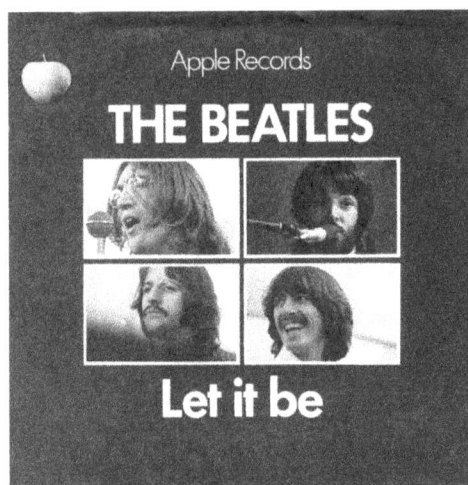

Apple Records *Let it Be* LP Cover

Sgt. Pepper's Lonely Hearts Club Band LP Cover

Rehearsal for *The Ed Sullivan Show*

Seth Kaller, Inc. invites you to experience the wonder of owning important historic documents. Our goal is to create a personal connection between you and your favorite historic event, figure, or idea. We specialize in finding rare items, with a particular focus on documents of significant content, which often are available for just a brief time and, once sold, may never come on the market again.

Documents that Seth has handled have since been exhibited at or acquired by The Smithsonian Institution, The National Constitution Center, Atlanta History Center, The Gettysburg National Civil War Museum, the New York Stock Exchange, Mount Vernon, The University of Virginia, Rice University, Yale University, the Skirball Cultural Center, The Kennedy Space Center, The Lincoln Museum, and several Presidential Libraries and National Parks museums, and other notable institutions.

Seth has represented the Gilder Lehrman Collection since its inception in 1989. The GLC, now at the New-York Historical Society, is among the most important American document collections ever privately formed. Seth's acquisitions for GLC include Benjamin Franklin's signed copy of the U.S. Constitution, George Washington's and Thomas Jefferson's letters on the war, religion, slavery, and government, Abraham Lincoln's "House Divided" Speech manuscript, and Robert E. Lee's signed farewell order to his troops.

Twenty-six Lincoln- signed copies of the "Authorized Edition" of the Emancipation Proclamation are known to survive. Since 1985, nine have been publicly offered. Seth Kaller has handled eight, including one that sold at Robert A Siegel Auction Galleries on June 26, 2012.

Portraits of George Washington by Gilbert Stuart and Rembrandt Peale, Jean-Antoine Houdon's bust of Thomas Jefferson, and Childe Hassam's flag painting, "Fourth of July, 1916," are among the important works of art Kaller has acquired for clients.

Today, Seth works with both private collectors and institutional clients, including museums, libraries, universities and foundations. He is available for private consultations, appraisals and authentications.

www.sethkaller.com

Seth Kaller, Inc

Historic Documents & Legacy Collections

PHONE 914-289-1776

FAX 914-289-1789

INFO@SETHKALLER.COM

A Visit from the Character Assassins, or How Handwriting Restored the Reputation of Clement C. Moore

By Seth Kaller

"Twas the night before Christmas, and all through the house..." I don't really have to go on, do I? You know the rest. *A Visit from St. Nicholas* is often called the world's most famous and beloved poem. The anonymity of its first publication, on December 23, 1823 in the *Troy Sentinel*, though, was something of an accident. The newspaper editor in upstate New York who had received a copy – perhaps even Moore's original manuscript – didn't learn who the author was until a few years later. But Clement Clarke Moore's authorship became known well before he himself published it in his 1844 book, *Poems*. His iconic verses created the modern vision of Santa Claus, a beautiful and captivating story at the center of holiday celebrations welcomed by Americans of every religion.

But every year, we read in various places that there is doubt about authorship. From where? Decades after Moore was univerally acknowledged as the author, a member of the Poughkeepsie-based Livingston family "recalled" that many years earlier, another family member "discovered" that "a mistake" had been made. The family member claimed that about 20 years before the *Troy Sentinel* got it, Henry Livingston had written and published the poem! The problem with this claim was that the single manuscript copy wass said to have been destroyed in a fire and the supposed Livingston publication has never been found. Neither has any evidence that Livingston himself claimed authorship. Still, the Livingston clan ramped up the campaign to re-attribute *The Night Before Christmas*. As specific details of their claims were discredited (for instance, the first ancestor said to have heard Livingston read the poen in 1808 died a few months before that could have happened,) the story evolved. Nothing stuck, so the Livingstons turned to *ad hominem* attacks. Unlike their beloved patriarch, they argued, Moore was a religiously bigoted and mean-spirited curmudgeon, a hater of fun who despised rambunctious children. Such a character, they argued, simply could not have written a light-hearted, child-friendly poem.

Enter Vassar College professor Don Foster's book *Author Unknown: On the Trail of Anonymous* (Holt, 2000). Foster admitted at the start that much of the Livingston story had already been disproven. Even so, he goes on to recycle it as fact, claiming that "linguistic forensics," his own foolproof method of detecting authorship, showed Livingston to be the true author. With an entirely complete series of counter-factual arguments that relied on cherry-picked and manipulated "evidence," Foster expanded on prior claims, and then went further, he found physical evidence proving that Moore was a serial plagiarist.

Here is where the handwriting finally comes in. Moore penned at least four holographic (entirely in his hand) manuscripts of A Visit from St. Nicholas. Three are now in institutions and can be found in The Strong Museum in Rochester, New York, The Huntington Library in California, and The New York Historical Society. At the time Foster's book came out, my family and I owned the fourth. With this connection to the handwritten copy, I had to learn more.

If Moore was proven to be a plagiarist, I would say that his writing of any number of copies was not sufficient to prove his authorship. Was he? According to Foster, a book about Merino sheep provided the answer. Moore had added to the book "*a handwritten note explaining how he happened to possess such a curious volume: he was himself the anonymous translator! ....he lays claim to an entire book that was the work of another man*" (Foster 273-4). Moore's "fraud" is then too easily exposed; the last page of the

book names the actual translator (Foster 273-4). It took no time for us to find the original book in question; it was given to The New York Historical Society around 1814, and was still there. The incriminating "handwritten note" turned out to be only the inscription "by Clement C Moore A.M." So, what claim did Moore really make in this incriminating note? None at all. The illustrations provided here for comparison prove that this damning case of plagiarism is entirely imaginary. Moore's name was *not* written by Moore. Perhaps his name was added by a clerk to credit Moore's gift of the book to The New York Historical Society. At worse, it shows that someone else thought Moore translated the work.

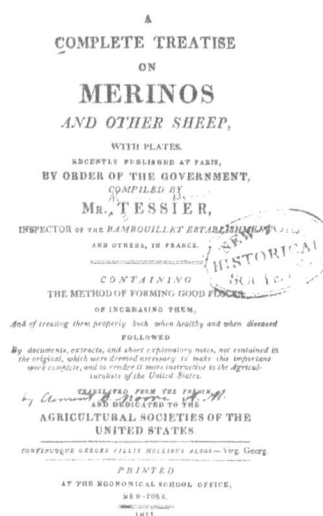

The "signed" book that the Livingstonians have used to call Moore a plagiarist.

Without physical evidence, though, there is still the question of character. Like Foster, Livingstonians depicted Clement Moore as a self-righteous, moralizing paragon of rectitude. He was incapable of writing *A Visit from St. Nicholas*, they argued, because he was a nasty, rich man who hated noisy kids, and by the way, his sons were all philanderers. According to Foster, Moore was "a grouchy pedant, a student of ancient Hebrew who never had a day of fun in his life. In fact he was against it" (Foster 227). Not the slightest bit of real evidence bears that out. For instance, Foster quotes one of Moore's letters to show that *"his own mother thought of him as a 'woman hater,' a scholar like 'the long-bearded Jew who [...] could love nothing but musty black-leather books'"* (Foster 247, ellipses Foster's). Handwriting again revealed the truth, when we checked Foster's quote against the young professor's original letter and discovered that his edited quote distorted the meaning: *"If you feel inclined to laugh at me for what I have written to you, what would you do if you could see me through such a magic glass as we read of in the Arabian Nights entertainment? The woman hater, the long-bearded Jew, who as you all supposed, or pretended to suppose could love nothing but musty black-leather books, is converted into as spruce & gallant a lady's man as you ever beheld...we ramble about in the country and talk all manner of nonsense; I cut her name upon the trees and try, without success, to make verses..."* (Moore to his mother, October 16, 1813, The New York Historical Society). Any objective observer can recognize that the phrase "pretended to suppose" (elided in Foster's quote) is a clue that Moore was kidding.

Cover of the famous illustrated edition published by McLoughlin Brothers, 1888

Thomas Nast, woodcut, published in Harper's Weekly, January 3, 1874

Thomas Nast, woodcut, published in Harper's Weekly, December 24, 1881

What about his child-hating, noise-obssessed ways? A passage from an unpublished holographic verse, written by Moore for his granddaughter in 1849, puts the lie to that: *"The house is all too dull and quiet;/I long to hear you romp and riot/When e'er you're full of harmless fun,/I dearly love to see you run"* (Misc. Moore, C.C. Coll. Museum of the City of New York).

And Moore's supposed abhorrence of spiritually un-useful verse, and of the veneration of saints? Foster writes, *"From Moore's point of view, Christmas was no time to be jolly, but a season for worship, for repentance from sin... When the evidence is laid out on the table, one cannot help but wonder how A Visit from St. Nicholas ever came to be associated with an old curmudgeon like Clement Clarke Moore in the first place"* (Foster 245; 266). Leaving aside Moore's many generous gifts to Saint Peter's Church, a holographic poem we found in the Museum of the City of New York completely puts the lie to that claim. Moore ghost wrote in this letter "From St. Nicholas" to ne of his daughters who was just learning to read. Predating A Visit, likely by only a year, it is, perhaps the first letter ever written by Santa Claus. Though not ready for prime time, it provides another major link in the story of the invention of the modern Santa.

And the "linguistic forensics" that scientifically prove Livingston to be the author? Dr. Joe Nickell, author of Pen, Ink and Evidence, pointed out in his thorough analysis, 'It is easy to fall into the trap of starting with the desired answer and working backward to the evidence, picking and choosing that which best fits" (Nickell, *Manuscripts*, Winter 2003, 10). Foster's selective linguistic analysis entirely disregards any evidence in favor of Moore's authorship. Lighthearted, spontaneous-sounding mixed iambs and anapests, exclamation marks, the "rare" use of "all" as an adverb, syncopation, familial affection – all of the linguistic evidence for Livingston can also be seen in the many lines written by Moore. And when discussing the origin of certain words or phrases, ("all snug," for example), Foster goes to tortuous lengths to create an association with Livingston, but ignores much more direct connections to Moore, including published and unpublished writings.

In his preface to a translation he made of Juvenal's Satire, Moore wrote that "no production which assumes the guise of poetry ought to be tolerated, if it possesses no other recommendation than the glow of its expressions and the tinkling of its syllables, or the wanton allurement of the ideas that it conveys." In the next sentence, though, he explains further: "It should be scrupulously required, that whenever words are put together, they be assembled for some rational purpose; that if the affections be addressed, the feeling intended to be excited be one of which human nature is susceptible; that if an image be presented to the imagination, its form be distinguishable; and that if reason be called upon, something be expressed which the mind can comprehend." (xxv-xxvi)

Moore scrupulously followed this poetic program when he later composed *The Night Before Christmas*. There was a rational purpose to this story: to entertain children, which providing (inventing) a bit of useful social history.

The feelings he addressed were so "susceptible" to human nature, that almost 200 years later the verse is still read and loved. The images he presented were so "distinguishable" that they have inspired countless paintings, drawings and prints, and even other poetry and songs.

I started my investigation with a willingness to let the chips fall where they might. In the end, any unbiased look at the evidence – documentary, historical and linguistic – must lead to the conclusion that Moore was indeed the work's author. When all the "personal opinions" and "personal rhetoric" of people are put aside, there is not a shred of real evidence supporting the anti-Moore, pro-Henry Livingston authorship case. Livingston may have been a great guy, who likely did write a long-forgotten Christmas poem – but he didn't write this one. Clement Clarke Moore, unjustly accused of falsely taking credit for the classic holiday poem, should be at rest, his reputation restored.

*** Seth Kaller dubunks additional anti-Moore arguments on his website, www.sethkaller.com ***

References:

Nickell, Joe, *New Yorker*, 23 Dec 2002.

Elliott, Jock 'A Ha! Christmas': An Exhibition at the Grolier Club of *Jock*

Elliot's Christmas Books, New York: The Grolier Club, 1999

Foster, Donald, *Author Unknown: On the Trail of Anonymous*, New York, Henry Holt and Company, 2000

Jones, Charles W., *Knickerbocker Santa Claus, New York Historical Society Quarterly* Volume 38 (Oct. 1954)

Moore, Clement Clarke, Papers at Columbia University Library, Museum of the City of New York, The New York Historical Society

Nickell, Joe, *The Case of the Christmas Poem, Manuscripts*, Fall 2002, and Part 2, Winter 2003

Nissenbaum, Stephen, *The Battle for Christmas: A Cultural History of America's Most Cherished Holiday*, New York, Vintage, 1996

A few of the signatures compared against the "signature" in the Merino book.

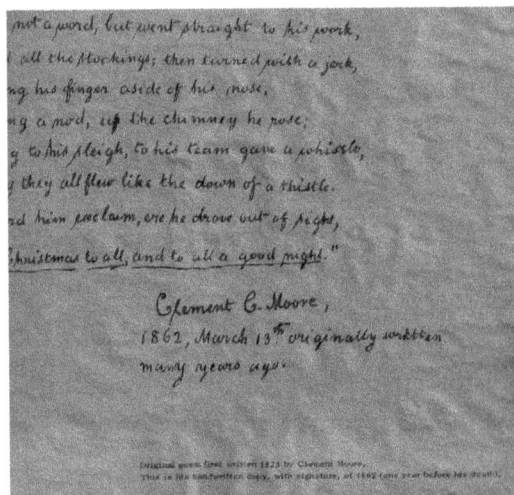

Facsimile of Moore's autographed manuscript signed and given to the New York Historical Society in 1862. We get many calls every year from people who ask us to authenticate these, thinking they have found an original. It pays to look at the fine print!

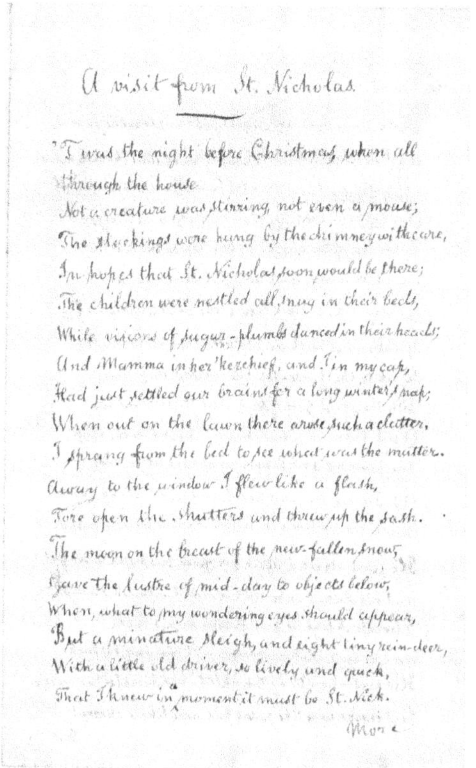

A visit from St. Nicholas.

'Twas the night before Christmas, when all
through the house
Not a creature was stirring, not even a mouse;
The stockings were hung by the chimney with care,
In hopes that St. Nicholas soon would be there;
The children were nestled all snug in their beds,
While visions of sugar-plums danced in their heads;
And Mamma in her 'kerchief, and I in my cap,
Had just settled our brains for a long winter's nap;
When out on the lawn there arose such a clatter,
I sprang from the bed to see what was the matter.
Away to the window I flew like a flash,
Tore open the shutters and threw up the sash.
The moon on the breast of the new-fallen snow,
Gave the lustre of mid-day to objects below,
When, what to my wondering eyes should appear,
But a miniature sleigh, and eight tiny rein-deer,
With a little old driver, so lively and quick,
That I knew in a moment it must be St. Nick.

Moore

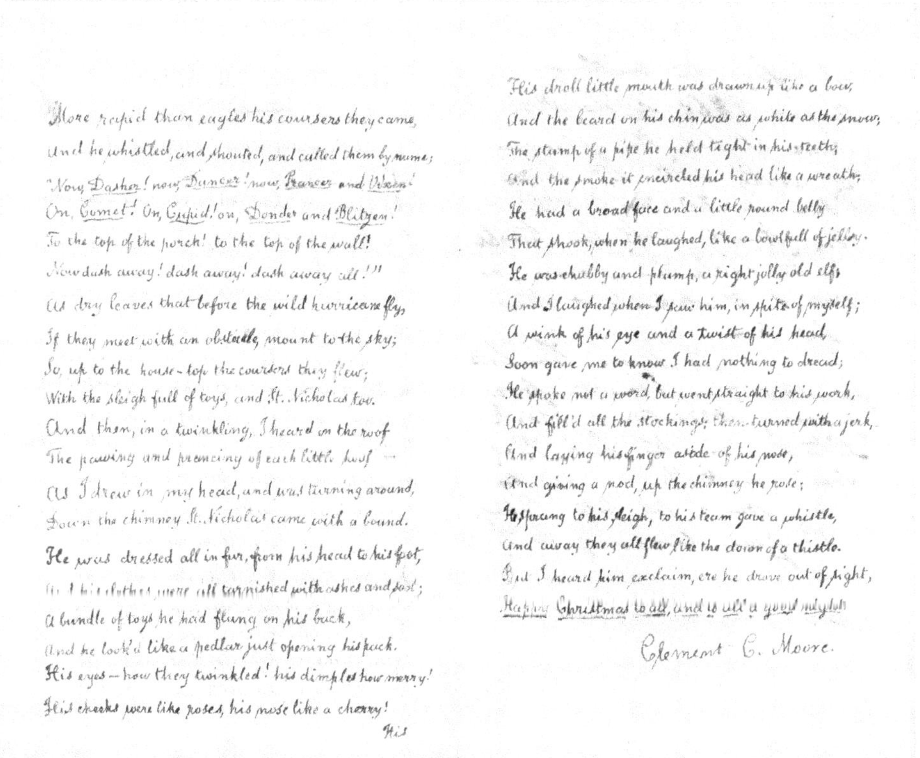

More rapid than eagles his coursers they came,
And he whistled, and shouted, and called them by name;
"Now, Dasher! now, Dancer! now, Prancer and Vixen!
On, Comet! On, Cupid! on, Donder and Blitzen!
To the top of the porch! to the top of the wall!
Now dash away! dash away! dash away all!"
As dry leaves that before the wild hurricane fly,
If they meet with an obstacle, mount to the sky;
So, up to the house-top the coursers they flew;
With the sleigh full of toys, and St. Nicholas too.
And then, in a twinkling, I heard on the roof
The prancing and pawing of each little hoof —
As I drew in my head, and was turning around,
Down the chimney St. Nicholas came with a bound.
He was dressed all in fur, from his head to his foot,
And his clothes were all tarnished with ashes and soot;
A bundle of toys he had flung on his back,
And he look'd like a pedlar just opening his pack.
His eyes — how they twinkled! his dimples how merry!
His cheeks were like roses, his nose like a cherry!
His

His droll little mouth was drawn up like a bow,
And the beard on his chin was as white as the snow;
The stump of a pipe he held tight in his teeth,
And the smoke it encircled his head like a wreath;
He had a broad face and a little round belly
That shook, when he laughed, like a bowl full of jelly.
He was chubby and plump, a right jolly old elf,
And I laughed when I saw him, in spite of myself;
A wink of his eye and a twist of his head,
Soon gave me to know I had nothing to dread;
He spoke not a word, but went straight to his work,
And fill'd all the stockings; then turned with a jerk,
And laying his finger aside of his nose,
And giving a nod, up the chimney he rose;
He sprang to his sleigh, to his team gave a whistle,
And away they all flew like the down of a thistle.
But I heard him exclaim, ere he drove out of sight,
Happy Christmas to all, and to all a good night.

Clement C. Moore.

Clement Clarke Moore's 1860 autograph manuscript signed

ICONOGRAPHS

Welcome to Iconographs! We are one of the largest dealers on the internet of In-Person, contemporary celebrity autographs! By far, the most important aspect in the purchase of autographs is the guarantee of an item's authenticity. Not only do all of our items come with a 10-day money back guarantee and lifetime certificates of authenticity, collectors will be hard pressed to find other autograph dealers who will offer that kind of provenance and match our prices too!

Iconographs currently employs more In-Person collectors on both coasts than any other internet dealer. Weekly packages are sent from our collectors containing the fruits of their labors, photos with the stars, and detailed information on exactly when and where each item was obtained.

Iconograph's agenda is simple, to offer a wide range of authentic, In-Person autographs at prices all collectors can afford. Our success on the internet tells us that we are accomplishing just that.

We now invite you to the new and improved Iconographs web site. So sit back, relax, and enjoy - there's a lot to see, and more importatnly, when you make your selections, you can do so with confidence and trust.

www.iconographs.com

ANDY GRIFFITH

The Definitive Signature Study of America's Favorite Television Sheriff

By Nelson Deedle

In July 2012, television fans across the world lost one of their heroes and a man with a great moral compass, Andy Griffith. Like so many, I grew up watching The Andy Griffith Show. When I started to collect autographs, at the age of 11, I naturally decided to form an Andy Griffith collection. Luckily, I started collecting early enough to have met many of the stars of the show who are now also deceased such as Don Knotts, Denver Pyle, George Lindsay, Jack Dodson, Howard Morris, Hal Smith, and even Andy himself.

Andy Griffith's authentic autograph is one of the rarest of all classic television stars that has been wrongly authenticated and sold in error for decades. After semi-retiring to a small town in North Carolina in the 1990s, Mr. Griffith was rarely seen in Los Angeles and New York. In fact, Griffith's hot show Matlock was moved to North Carolina in 1993 so Mr. Griffith didn't have to commute to Universal City, California, where the previous seasons had been filmed.

When asked to sign autographs in person, Andy Griffith was always a reluctant signer, often pretending like he didn't hear the request. To complicate matters, Griffith suffered from crippling arthritis and a nerve disorder called Guillain-Barre Syndrome, which almost killed him in 1983. However, while Andy wasn't accommodating in person, collectors had tremendous "luck" getting his autograph by writing him through the mail. This doesn't make sense until after examination an overwhelming majority of the mail autographs were secretarial.

It is widely believed that Mr. Griffith's manager, Richard O. Linke, acted as his ghost signer for most of Mr. Griffith's career. Mr. Linke was a controlling gatekeeper to Mr. Griffith and everything went through him. Mr. Griffith once said, "If there is ever a question about something, I will do what he wants me to do. Had it not been for him, I would have gone down the toilet."

The autograph market has been so diluted with secretarial Andy Griffith autographs that an authentic Griffith autograph can be had for under $100, which is a bargain! A signed cut can be had for around $30-$40, signed 8x10 for $80-$120, signed check for $75-$100, and signed contract for $200-$300.

Once you know what to look for, authentic Andy Griffith autographs can be spotted immediately.

Andy Griffith's authentic autograph has a free flowing style.

Andy Griffith signature on the playbill for "No Time for Sergeants"

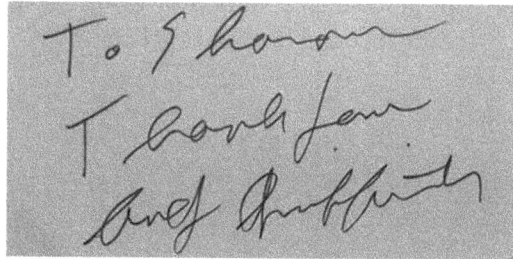

Selection of authentically signed photos

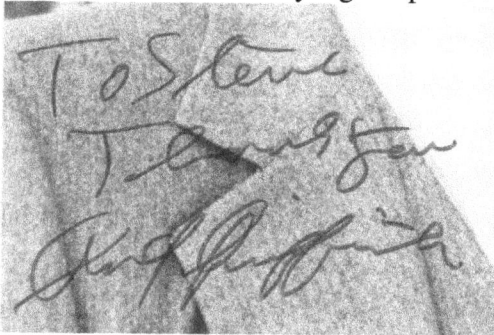

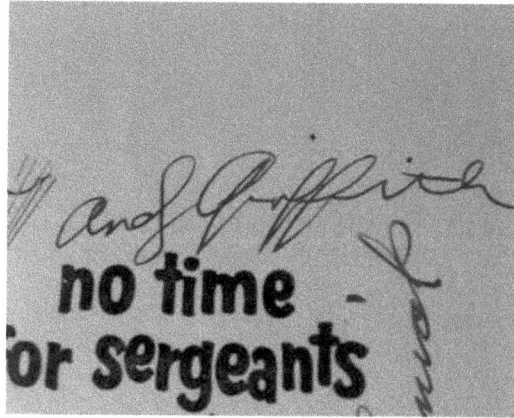

Authentic inscription and signature

Selection of authentically signed checks

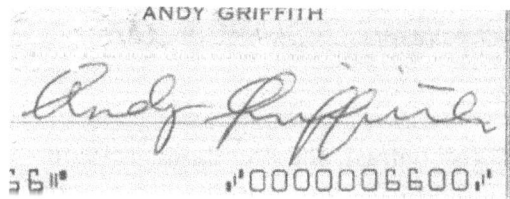

Andy Griffith Enterprises
authentically signed contract

An endorsed check signed by both Andy
Griffith and Richard O. Linke

Photo of Andy Griffith signing

In contrast, the secretarial version of Andy Griffith's autograph is more ridged and is formed in a completely different style.

The easiest way to tell if you are looking at a secretarial is to examine the "ith" of Griffith. Andy's ghost signer always, without exception, looped the "th" back to touch the "ff" in Griffith. Andy never did this.

The secretary always formed a solid "A" in Andy and "G" in Griffith starting the pen stroke from the top. Andy always started his pen stroke from the bottom on both letters, often crossing out both letters as a result.

Selection of secretarial signatures

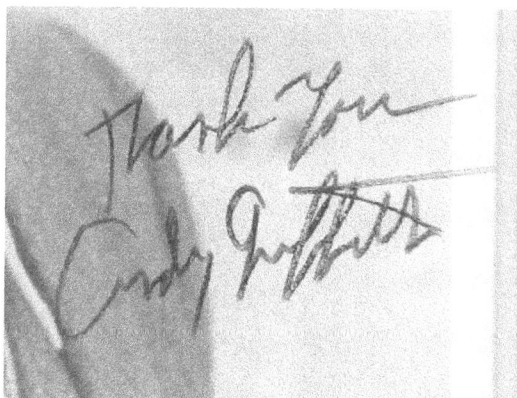

awful arthritis." Seeing the look of disappointment on our faces, he suggested that he could try to make "his mark." His mark turned out to be an "X." It was better than nothing.

He happily posed for photos and thanked us for recognizing him. As he left he said, "I'm having dinner with Ron (Howard) tonight. I bet that's a photo you'd like to have." We said "YES!" and asked him where they were going. "Oh no you don't," he laughed.

The Andy Griffith Show

The last time I saw Andy Griffith was a few years before his death. He was in Los Angeles on business staying at the Peninsula Hotel in Beverly Hills. With several friends in tow, we went over to see him. He seemed generally thrilled to see us and asked what we wanted. When we asked for him to sign our photographs he said, "I can't, I have

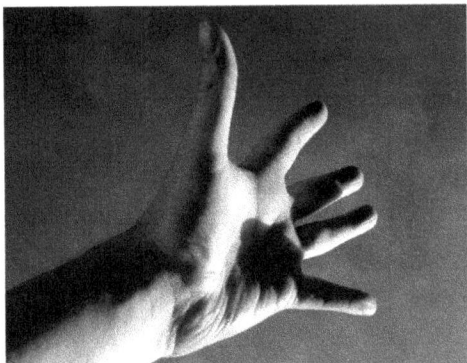

Scions of Science Fiction

By Philip Marsh

"Logic will take you from A to B.
Imagination will take you everywhere."
Albert Einstein

Science Fiction can be considered our dreams come to life. Whether in pulp, book or movie form it takes delight in showing what could be done with the right futuristic inventions and the trouble that follows when left in the hands of humans just beginning to figure out how to handle it. The stories were always innovative, ground breaking, thought provoking, and endlessly fascinating, just like the authors themselves. Their backgrounds were as divergent as the stories they created, yet they couldn't have been more alike in their goals to wake up a sentient world to an emerging Sci-Fi genre and keep it awake for generations to come.

Jules Gabriel Verne, Herbert George Wells, Hugo Gernsback, Edgar Rice Burroughs, Forrest J. Ackerman, and Philip K. Dick were entertaining storytellers, artists with writing quills, and each one tells us there's a practical moral to be learned somewhere in their artwork. Some invented it, some made it grow, some expanded on it, and others took it in different directions. It's one invention we've got figured out.

"Anything one man can imagine, other men can make real."
Jules Verne

The emerging Sci-Fi genre took place between wildly different authors of divergent backgrounds and approaches.

Jules Gabriel Verne (1828-1905) will always be remembered by a grateful reading populace as being a French writer of fantastic journeys, graphic tales of future inventions and stories of eventual society changes. Jules Verne predicted entire generations, hundreds of years in the future. By taking a close look at his books and articles we can see he had an unmatched gift for seeing down the road of time and being able to tell in which direction the world would be turning in a dizzying array of subjects, from the center of the earth to the Moon and back. The author's work was prophetic, cloaked in adventure telling, bringing in technology which seemed farfetched in its day, yet in years to come would become the norm. After Dame Agatha Christie, he would go on to become the second most translated author in the world. Jules Verne consistently is in the top five most translated authors of the world.

Verne came from a well to do family, with a father who worked as a lawyer. When they visited their summer house just outside the city of Nantes, the coming and going of the large schooners and cargo ships sparked his interest and it wasn't long before he was imagining great exploration with travel as a predominant theme in his works such as *Journey to the Center of the Earth*, *20,000 Leagues Under the Sea*, *Around the World In Eighty Days*, and *Mysterious Island*. The formula usually involved characters going off on the trip of a lifetime, getting involved with situations that were possible, though usually highly abnormal. They operated in a closed setting trying to adjust, and ultimately triumph, over high odds. Verne's father, wishing for him to follow in the family tradition of being in

law, sent him to Paris. Verne promptly indulged his liking to develop libretti for operettas, as well as his true talent, that of writing incredible voyages with details on traveling and lands that would charm the public. His father was not amused to find out his son wasn't following his recommended course of study, and promptly cut off his money. Undeterred, Verne went to work as a stockbroker, which he could do despite the fact he detested the work. But after he had gotten a taste of writing at an early age about the type of life he so greatly loved, he would never be content with a workaday existence.

He had found his calling, and setting crow quill to vellum was a better occupation than reading Detinues or wrestling with *Mesne Profits*. In 1867, he would buy a small ship, the Saint-Michel and replace it with others as his money continued to grow. He would use it to sail around Europe, but his real ship for traveling turned out to be his imagination, filled to the rafters with gallons of imagination for fuel, the starched sails set out with a healthy snap to the line when a strong story wind beckoned, and a rudder made up of opinion and facts that would enable him to chart an unerring course to the intellectual islands in the stream he was forever dreaming about and sailing to. The boats may have been small, but it was probably one of the few times in history millions of people climbed on board and got a ride they would never forget.

Verne actually had trouble getting his works into bookstores until he met Pierre-Jules Hetzel, an influential French publisher. On his advice, comedy was added, political messages were cut back, and happy endings were accented. Verne's output increased to two volumes a year, and with the wealth from the stage adaptations, he could now live on his writings alone. No doubt his father could now be happy on the successful direction his son's life took in a chancy and competitive field. Like most of Sci-Fi's writers today, his works were looked upon as adventures with fantastical notions of mechanical inventions or impossible changes in the structure of society as we know it. Verne predicted submarines, air travel, glass skyscrapers, and even landing on the moon. The success with Science Fiction writers in being able to correctly assume what events in society, such as calculators, and new traveling inventions seems to be very high, higher than any psychics. Getting a prediction right on nothing but chance is considered 25%. By examining Verne's projections, it's clear he's far ahead even using today's standards. He was a visionary, observing the modern world and making educated predictions where science will take us hundreds, even thousands of years in the future. Verne not only predicted one day man would walk on the moon, but the similarity in *From the Earth to the Moon* had to the American space effort was too close to be brushed off. His account specifically told how it was done from a launch pad in Florida to the pickup out in the ocean. *20,000 Leagues* pitched the idea of a clean, renewable energy source-water. Like most writers with a long list of predictions, one of them took longer than ever to come true, but Hydrogen Fuel Cell technology is getting closer every day to replacing fossils. Verne's narratives predicted cataclysmic world wars and the horrors that would come with them. From chemical warfare to

weapons of mass destruction, unbelievably to the rise of a popular German statesman bent on world domination, Verne had foresight that had to be the envy of writers and crystal ball readers around the world. From a distance of over a hundred years, he described television, computer, and a culture that would find itself addicted to an internet. The written guesses of Nostradamus were nowhere as close as a Science Fiction writer from France. Perhaps the question we should ask of ourselves now is this: since we have aged 150 years since he made his most famous predictions, can we now, even with all the scientific knowledge that has come to pass, manage to come up with even one person like Verne that would be able to make such a skilled and accurate set of speculations to come?

In 1905, while ill with Diabetes, Verne passed away. Perhaps one of the most unbelievable things that would happen was when Verne wrote *Paris au XXe Siecle* or *Paris in the Twentieth Century* in 1863. It contained future wonders such as high speed trains, automobiles powered by gasoline, helicopters and airplanes. But his good friend Hetzel wanted more optimism to the plot lines and suggested he wait for twenty years before publishing it. Verne put it in a safe where it wasn't discovered until his great grandson found it in 1989, a staggering 123 years later. It was published in 1994, much to the delight of Verne and Science Fiction fans alike.

It's doubtful we'll ever see his like again. Even though he is one of many predicting writers, he was still one-of-a-kind, in a class of his own. You could rightfully say he was responsible for creating a new type of thinking, one that involved the unlikely meld of prophetic story with science inventions that certainly must have seemed Godlike to the majority of his readers. It could have easily been properly labeled Science-Future. His approach is timeless and good stories know no national boundaries. They can be made into movies with a different slant or bent and a new crew each generation. They still look fresh and have something to offer to the new or returning reader. Verne, a storyteller of science, created the adventure, but has stayed on our bookshelves because the viewing public were the ones that took the trip.

"Civilization is a race between education
and catastrophe."
H.G. Wells

When special effect laden movies with superstar actors began to take over the cinema, it became inevitable producers would reach back to the classics that had been made from international best seller's decades earlier. By twisting the story and injecting modern day problems that would impress an experienced movie public, yet more money could be wrung out of a story that had many fathers;

prediction, despair mixed with optimism, socio-political commentary and a society thousands of years old that was still experiencing growth pangs. It's easy to do when the story has stood the test of time, such as the case with prolific English author Herbert George Wells (1866-1946).

Although Wells beginnings were more Dickensian than privilege, his writing never reflected the abysmal poverty he was raised in. He was born in Bromly, near London. Wells' desire to write came about as a result of an accident in 1874, in which he was laid up with a broken leg. Looking to keep his mind active, his father would bring him books from the public library, which whetted his appetite for more. His world consisted of faraway lands, different customs never dreamed of, people never imagined. His temporary layup sparked his imagination to write himself. Life gave him a lemon, and he created a worldwide demand for his lemonade.

His parents were poor, and Wells was forced to drop out of school and become apprenticed to a draper at 14. Although he won a scholarship to the Normal School of Science in 1883, he was forced to leave because of financial reasons. When he went to live with his Aunt and Uncle Wells on Fitzroy Road in London, he began liaisons with an uncounted number of other women, some of whom were the direct inspiration for characters in his books. In 1890, Wells earned his bachelor's in Zoology from the University of London. He went on to secure a teaching position where he taught A.A. Milne, who would go on to write about a certain golden bear and his adolescent friends in the hundred acre woods.

Whereas Verne's novels were closer to 19th century adventure stories, Wells books were more scholarly in nature, asking questions of society regarding a wide span of issues. To get a greater idea of what was going on in Wells' mind as well as understanding what the real themes of the story were, it's good to take off the top layer of some of his most successful efforts and get a deeper look. When you take a closer glimpse at what he wrote about, you get a more detailed picture of the man.

The first novel by Wells, *The Time Machine*, (1895) has the hero transported into the year 802, 701. The world as the scientist traveler knew it is long gone, now peopled by two groups, an extreme upper class, and even more extreme lower class. The two classes would be given their names from the Biblical Eli and Moloch. It's a trip into the future, all right, a supreme example of what happens when capitalism goes without checks and balances. A daydreaming and irresponsible above-ground race called Eloi become dependent on the combination caveman and gorilla underground dwellers known as the dreaded Morlocks. The Eloi, numbed to an almost unconscious degree represent the upper class that is at first nurtured, then eventually eaten by a class of proletariat driven to the depths of existence. The hero, after defeating the Morlock, is now left with a question: With what do you replace capitalism?

Wells' writing seems inevitably to mix in several themes at once, such as 1896's *The Island of Doctor Moreau*, which took on themes of eugenics, religion, the right, or wrong of scientific experimentation, and Darwin's idea of evolution. The lesson is clear; it will take a great deal of wisdom to play God and succeed. If natural selection does exist, then man could evolved up, or down, right? In a way, it's a version of Frankenstein as it asks, *"What makes us human?" "What keeps us separate from other animals?"* Since advocates for animal research and genetic manipulation invariably stay in the headlines, it makes for fascinating speculation as you walk thru the disturbing walls of the compound with the conscienceless Dr. Moreau, and meet many of his creations, some of them successful. After a while, the line between human and animal becomes blurred till there really isn't a line at all. Perhaps unintentionally, the book also becomes an argument about racism. If the idea switches from color to race, it still remains the same; should differing 'animals' be kept separate for their own good? Since most of Wells' work includes the insistent shout for social reform, it should come as no surprise in *Moreau* it works as a quiet undercurrent, much like the lapping of the waves in the ill-fated island lab. It's an old idea; a house without a good foundation won't stand.

Here, the house of experimentation works only as long as the natives don't get restless. Once they wise up, the house-and the ideas that built it-come crashing to the ground. His final point is mankind is doomed in advance when they try to change things that shouldn't be tampered with, and there are some subjects that shouldn't be tried. Scientists everywhere involved in cloning must have interesting opinions about the novel.

The Invisible Man (1897) is like many of Wells' writings; scratch the surface, and you'll liable to come away with a deeper meaning than you thought. The scientist named Griffin learns how to achieve transparency, but at the cost of losing his mind when he finds he can't change back and goes on a reign of terror. The invisible theme here, and this should come as no surprise from a socialist writer, is that there is a class structure in Britain, and there are many forgotten or *invisible* men and women in society. We see the seeds of rebellion being sown when a society's government creates and condemns itself with the same system of organization. It was an update of the *Ring of Gyges* by Plato, and modernization of a ring to a scientific idea. If Plato's hero Glaucon believed that "...injustice is far more profitable to the individual than justice," more than thousands of years ago, does the same idea apply no matter what the age? His point is morality comes from society, and it's mixed in with political themes, this one being the nameless poor. In any successful society, it's very likely the invisible man or woman will always be around.

The War of the Worlds (1898) - This is the granddaddy of all alien invasion stories. Make no mistake, however, it's a thickly made up attack on British imperialism. Like *The Time Machine*, Wells, who considered himself a socialist, is urging the reader to be able to look down the road of time and confront what will happen if complacency takes over the political scene and the invisible men and women are ruled by ennui instead of responsibility. It is typical Wells writing the protagonist is a learned man or scientist, a favorite technique in several of his writings. Mankind is surviving in the landscape of a cold and clinical government, who are headed to a slow train (or maybe saucer) crash, chilling to the point of unimaginability. Its galaxy imperialism, a holocaust outsweeping the Nazi's on a worldly scale. The Martians, as the invading race, do worse than chaos on a national scale; they're here to suck the blood out of the humans. They're not being managed so much as corralled. The analogy to the masses being sheeple for a controlling, all-powerful government is unavoidable.

Wells started off as being an world entertainer, became a teacher, then finally a lecturer, with the Earth as his lecture hall. Wells was also a prolific author is many other fields as well, being considered a futurist, historian, and socialist. In writing these stories and expressing his political views, he became a dichotomy. He was an optimist to believe in what he created, and he was a pessimist in believing the human race simply couldn't handle what he foresaw as inevitable courses of history unless a miracle was to change it.

Wells is on record as believing that World War II would start in 1940. He was only off by a matter of four months. Towards the end of WWII, Wells was alerted by the Allies. The Nazi's Operation Sea Lion, a plan abandoned when Germany failed to bomb England into submission, had a list of all undesirables to be rounded up, and most likely, disposed of as being enemies of the new regime. It turned out Wells' name was on it, because of actions he took as president of the Poets, Essayists, and Novelists Society. Because the German PEN club refused to admit writers of a non-Aryan nature, Wells expelled them. The Germans had long memories and forgave nothing. Wells and leading feminist and prolific author Rebecca West narrowly escaped being shipped over to Der Fatherland and assigned to a detention camp for extermination.

Wells passed away in 1946. Looking back, he will undoubtedly be remembered not only as an individual who tried to point out society's mistakes, but as someone who did what was right, not just accepted for that time. Although other authors would be remembered for espousing civil liberties such as women's rights, it's doubtful there were very many like Wells who had riots held by dissenters, trying to get people to not buy his books. Nothing excites a crowd more than an idea that goes against the grain, and makes more sense than a safe old time belief. He firmly believed mankind wasn't smart enough to stay out of trouble. He did believe though, we were smart enough to bump ourselves off. He was a prophet, a pessimist, a stern teacher who kept pushing the same theme throughout his life-"Either we wise up or we'll be the cause of our own troubles." Sometimes progress is like medicine; it may be good for you, but that doesn't mean you can get people to take it.

It was a theme he would return to again and again over his lifetime, in the hopes mankind would realize progress must be evaluated not by how powerful we can make our bombs, but how powerful our education is. Like Verne and Burroughs, his stories and points were perfectly suited to the limitless settings of Science-Fiction, where themes could be expanded no end, where the plots could infinitely be stretched, and mankind's ingenuity would be pushed to the ends of the galaxy to find a solution.

'The Country of the Blind', is a textbook example of that. It concerns a traveler who gets separated from his friends and encounters a race of people that gradually lost their sight too many years ago to count. They don't believe in this power called sight, and they think the traveler crazy for thinking he has another sense beyond the people that live in the extreme isolation of the village. Here the question is raised: If people say something exist, and it can't be 'seen' or felt or in any way confirmed, does that mean it doesn't exist? Wells' writing raised disturbing issues that were becoming more real every day, but perhaps the most disturbing effect of his stories was the fact that to some questions, the old beliefs were no longer any good and for a new age, there were no new answers.

If he were alive today, given his track record, there's a good chance he'd be championing gay rights, space travel and nuclear disarmament. Enthusiasts of Dungeon and Dragons dice games can also thank Wells for this: he was also the father of Miniature War Gaming and predicted robotics, World Wars, aerial bombing, as well as nuclear power.

Since movie spectacles over a hundred year history shows us the cinema only gets better with time, we can only wait to see what a future update of some of Wells' ideas will look like. Missing a modern version of a Verne or Ackerman, we can only look wistfully into our crystal balls known as word processors, wave the mouse wand, and make a wish. One prediction we can all make, that *will* come true, is that another reboot will be made. You can be assured if the same story is followed, then the same cinematic success will fill theatre coffers as the earlier hardback versions that were sold in bookstores over one hundred years ago. Now there's an invasion we can all look forward to.

"Let it be understood, in the first place, that a science fiction story must be an exposition of a scientific theme and it must be also a story."
Hugo Gernsback (1884-1967)

Cordially yours,

Like other gifted individuals, Gernsback was multi talented, an inventor, author, editor, publishing giant, and business owner. It's fair to refer to every one of the authors listed as being a futurist. But Gernsback also understood the mechanics of making money with savvy business intent in the magazine field, and used that for a springboard to financial independence.

Gernsback was born in Bonnevoie, Luxembourg City, Luxembourg. His father, Gernsbacher, wanted him to join the family business but science fascinated Hugo to a life changing degree. When he was younger, a technician at his father's winery showed him how to make a doorbell by hooking a battery together with a bell. He would look back at this as being the epiphany in his life, causing him to attend Electrical Engineering schools in Bingham, Germany. While still a teenager, he became an inventor as well as an author by inventing the first home radio set. Gernsback studied English in Brussels so he could pore over stories of the American West. In 1904 he set sailed for what he saw as the promised land of America. His initial interest lay in the import of radio parts and popularizing amateur 'wireless.' In 1908 he published the first magazine about radio called "Modern Electronics." When he founded the Wireless Association of America, it had 10,000 members in one year. In 1926 he brought this experience to dedicate an entire magazine dedicated to Science Fiction, appropriately named *Amazing Stories*.

Like Thomas Edison before him, inspiration with a seemingly limitless enthusiasm seemed to jump out at him from all corners. Like others who based a life and job on firm principles of test and prove, Gernsback had no patience with astrology, so called mystical tom foolery or the guesswork of cold reading psychics. Gernsback's predictions actually did come true on cell phones, computer dating, fax machines, flat screen television, fluorescent lighting, flying saucers, loudspeakers, microfilm, night baseball, plastics, radar guidance systems, sky writing, tape recorders, virtual reality, and more. His insight also led him to speculate on when the first manned moon landing would take place. He came close, saying it would be in the 1970's. Placing his reliance on scientific evolution enabled him, like

Verne and Wells, to come up with a stunningly high list of predictions that came true.

Science Fiction caught on for several reasons, but probably mostly because people love to speculate what the next thing will be in an ever changing society. What was fiction today could be cold hard fact tomorrow. That fact was driven home by Gernsback shrewdly cross promoting his own magazines and later using his radio stations to promote ideas he had written about in those same magazines.

Maybe it was his worship of earlier Serbian American inventor Nikola Tesla, who ideas and principles helped him to invent the alternating current electrical supply system, that helped spur Gernsback on to such ambitious projects. When Tesla collapsed and passed away from a coronary thrombosis, lifelong friend Gernsback commissioned a lifemask taken of Tesla, and published the picture in an issue of his *Practical Electronics* magazine. Before ending up in the Tesla Museum in Belgrade, Gernsback would keep the statue face in his office, in a special section for years.

He created the term "science fiction" although it could have turned out different. His preferred name of choice for a stories structure that consisted of "75 percent literature interwoven with 25 percent science" was "scientifiction." Fans could now organize because Gernsback started publishing letters with names and full addresses. Gernsback took in a staggering one hundred thousand dollars a year while being president of Gernsback Publications. During his life, he was to edit or publish no less than a staggering 54 magazines,

ranging from Science and Mechanics to Dreaming and French Humor. Writers working for his rock bottom commissions included inventive horror writer H.P. Lovecraft, Tarzan creator Edgar Rice Burroughs, and self taught horror and fantasy writer Clark Ashton Smith.

The magazines seemed to break new ground everywhere. He was no less talented as an inventor. At the time of his death in New York City in 1967 at the age of 87, he held 80 patents for radio and other electronic ideas. Whereas other authors were able to *look* into the future and predict with a staggering success rate the way society would turn, Gernsback concentrated on the machines that would help take us to the next technological milestone. They could have been named Hugostones; for his dogged efforts, he became known by his peers as the man that *invented* the future.

Because he was such a tireless crusader for science and critical thinking with imagination, no less a periodical than *Life* referred to him as being "the P.T. Barnum of the Space Age." While Gernsback certainly demonstrated a genius for being able to merchandise his interests in the inventions of the future, he was also tri-lingual and dressed in a manner considered by the press of the day as being debonair. His pioneering inventions included the direction finder, fluorescent lighting, micro film, stainless steel, tape records, and two way televisions. Combine marketing genius with a talent for future inventions and you're likely to not get a circus promoter with a reputation for hucksterism, but a creator of a whole new genre of reading.

Like Verne and Wells before him, an amazingly high amount of his prognostications came true. These included birth control, computer dating, cphones, fax machines, fluorescent lighting, language translators, loudspeakers, microfilm, night baseball, plastics, flat screen television, sky writing, tape recorders, and virtual reality. For his efforts, the Grand Duchess Charlotte of Luxembourg awarded him the "Officer of the Oaken Crown" in 1953. By then thrice married Gernsback would have the honor of the SF annual Science Fiction Achievement award named after him, and became a member of the SF Hall of fame. When he passed away in 1967 at the age of 83, the New York Times wrote not only about him as an author, inventor, and publisher, but referred to him as 'father of science fiction'.

His output was prodigious, his ideas ahead of their time and his perception of the way that new inventions, made possible by technology that had yet to be invented, were to affect our life was startling to say the least. Although primarily known as a publisher and inventor, his output with a huge and varied assortment of magazines, most of which stressed practical applications with electricity could be said to rival the prolific turnout of many nowadays authors. When you consider navigational guidance systems came about as a result of a child seeing a connecting wire touched to a battery, the outcome is even more astounding. In fact, some would say its pure science fiction.

"If I had followed my better judgment always, my life would have been a very dull one."

Edgar Rice Burroughs (1875-1950)

If by now you point out that only learned and college educated men were destined to create and define the role of S/F, then you would be even more startled to learn the background of *Tarzan* creator and the *John Carter of Mars* series. He was born in Chicago to civil war veteran George Tyler Burroughs and wife Mary Evaline Zieger Burroughs. His middle name came from his grandmother, Mary Rice Burroughs. Since outbreaks of diseases such as the influenza were sweeping the city, his parents decided to pack him off to a safer place; his brother's cattle ranch in Idaho. It was still a lawless place, and Burroughs met his share of bindlestiffs, gutterpups, and killers. It was a great place for a future author to gather information about future characters. A trip to town might even yield a rustler or two and it wasn't uncommon to witness a shootout at the local saloon. Burroughs loved every minute of it. Even though he took to it and embraced the wild and unpredictable West, his parents eventually found out about it and brought him back. The sporting life was replaced by being sent to the Phillips Academy, and then the Michigan Military Academy. He was unable to join West Point after failing the entrance exam. He wound up as an enlisted man in the 7th Cavalry, Custer's previous unit, but was discharged after a physical showed he had a heart problem. After working a series of low paying and dead end jobs, he wound up as, of all things, a pencil sharpener wholesaler. Work days were not exactly filled with the type of excitement he saw on an almost daily basis in the wild Idaho country.

Most of the time, he would wait for his sharpener salesmen to show up and check magazines to see if their advertisements were published. At age 35, his life was to parallel *Wizard of Oz* creator L. Frank Baum in that it was failure followed by failure, until one of his creations struck it big. He wound up reading a great deal, pulp S/F among the top of the list. Burroughs just could not get over the writers for these magazines got paid for typing what he termed 'rot' and knew he could write a better story than them, even though he had never written one of that type in his life. He was an immediate hit, selling his first story "Under the Moons of Mars" to *All-Story Magazine* in 1912. He actually used the non de plume of 'Norman Bean' instead of his real name so no one would recognize who really wrote the story. When the money went up, so did his name on the front. The covers often were made up of nightmare creatures from your imagination to grab the bystander's eye and lure them closer. His first effort brought him four hundred dollars, a huge sum for those days, and equal to about nine thousand dollars nowadays. The publishers and the public couldn't get enough of him, and his characters were so restless he needed several new worlds for them to roam. His third novel introduced a Lord of British descent that preferred dressing in lion skin to suits, and the legend of

Tarzan was introduced. Inspired, and not one to miss a writing angle, Burroughs began to turn out prehistoric stories, social matters, inner world, horror stories, lost at sea stories and westerns. This included Venus and other rugged places he had seen firsthand on the wild plains of Idaho. He was so successful he began writing full time. Because *Tarzan* was such an immediate success, Burroughs worked out a media plan that would exploit *Tarzan* into the public consciousness as never before. Rationalizing that popularity of one product would draw attention to and increase sales of other product, *Tarzan* was made into movies, comic strips, merchandise and the sky high sells helped to bring a higher profit to his S/F works, including the earlier *Mars* and later *Venus* series. His books even outsold all his contemporaries such as Fitzgerald, Faulkner, and Hemingway. It was quite a long way for a former pencil sharpener manager to go.

The formula was one that would never grow old. It was to take the reader on a trip to new and uncharted lands, populate it with heroes and villains that were perhaps not all book educated, but educated in life, then fill it with a feeling of derring-do and high action. Burroughs would show how a population rises, how society divides, and how war spreads. When he pointed to *Mars* or *Venus*, he was actually pointing to Earth. Burroughs was showing how we were in danger of returning to tribalism. The public has never gotten tired of it. *Tarzan* was introduced in 1913 and is still in print today. Critics sometimes attacked Burroughs novels as savagely as the western Indians or four-armed martians he wrote about. They denounced his books as crudely written and chauvinistic. But the fact remains art is done for the money, and money is the judge of the art. The written art in this case is just as valuable and more as anything seen in the Louvre, perhaps more so. The masterpieces he created were painted with typewriter ribbon and ambition. If it's also true that authors tend to project themselves into their characters, then Burroughs successfully came up with several different projections of himself the public loved to read. Any effort could be attacked on strickly classical yardsticks, but that type of criticism grows weaker as the years, in this case centuries, roll on and the money continues to accumulate. S/F has a relevance to present day, and perhaps the reason is the strong imagery and mythology Burroughs placed in his stories. To be able to claim a relevancy for over one hundred years is a neat publishing feat for any author to accomplish, and certainly does tend to batter any critic's claims about the quality of writing. Any writer or artist will agree, when all is said and done, only that which is good survives.

No less an individual than Ray Bradbury says, "Burroughs is probably the most influential writer in the history of the world." He went on to elaborate that most scientists grew up reading Burroughs and it influenced their occupation, eventually putting us on the moon. That's quite an achievement for a former pulp magazine writer and its creator to have influenced the world's most successful space program. Readers the world over can take no small amount of pride in knowing for each dime or dollar they put down to read such a magazine, it would lead to the influence of a man landing on a celestial body.

There are literally thousands of niche magazines in existence today, but very few that could lay claim to an honor like that. The space program started when geekheads for S/F put their money down for pulp magazines and books.

Burroughs had large ambitions and like Gernsback, a large drive to make them real. Possessed of a restless drive, in 1916 he took his wife Emma, their children, and their dog Tarzan on a camping trip across the country. They ended up in California where he bought a large ranch in 1919 north of Los Angeles, and named it Tarzana. In 1923, convinced he could make even greater profit, he set up his own printing company and published his books himself. Still not content to sit at home and collect royalty checks when the first movie *Tarzan* with sound came out in 1940, Burroughs and second wife Florence Dearholt headed farther west to Hawaii. Their son, Hulbert came out in 1941 to visit them, and was playing tennis with his dad when the Japanese flew over and bombed nearby Pearl Harbor. The last adventure in ERB's life just flew in.

When WWII broke out, he was 66 years old. Burroughs enlisted in the armed forces and became the oldest war correspondent working for the US during the war. On occasion he would bump into Hulbert who was working as a war photographer. When the war ended, he went back to Tarzana and settled in to a comfortable life turning out books plus numerous articles. He ended up publishing almost 70 books by the time of his death in 1950 of a heart attack.

Astronomers and any fan of the genre looking to the heavens can also spot a unique honor given to ERB - the Burroughs Crater on the planet Mars was given his name. How nice to think when we look up towards the stars, we're also looking in the same direction one of the most prolific authors of S/F set his adventures and the inspiration of many stories. Fortunately for us, looking out and past worldly limitations has always been a forte of dreamers and S/F writers.

"Take me home young man.
You will love me!"
Forrest J Ackerman, when he picked up his first S/F magazine at age nine.

The advancement of Science Fiction out of yellowing pulp magazines and low budget black and white movies into the modern day bound volumes and digital CGI films cannot be passed over without the inclusion of Sci-Fi's biggest fan, Forrest J (no dot after the initial) Ackerman. He was a tireless writer's agent, the ultimate collector, who never gave up thinking young. He was known to the fans as Uncle Forry, Mr. Science Fiction, Dr. Ackula, 4E, 4SJ, the Ackermonster, Sgt. Ack Ack, but perhaps no other name suited him better than, 'Number one fan in all of moviedom.' For over eight decades, he was the epitome of S/F's three S's: supporter, spokesman, and salesman. The S/F could have stood for Super Forry.

He was born Forrest Clark Ackerman in 1916 and grew up in Los Angeles. "In those days magazines spoke," explained Forry. The life-changing one that happened to speak to young Ackerman was a September 1926 *Amazing Stories*, edited by none other than Hugo Gernsback. He took it home all right, and soon his life was to be tied to a rocket ship of fantasy and launched to the outer limits of the S/F entertainment world.

As a youngster, Forrest would see sometimes up to seven S/F movies in one day, all with the support of his parents. By the age of ten, Forry was already mailing his opinion to national publications and movie studios. Back in the thirties and forties, anyone who paid as much attention to the genre was thought to be a bit peculiar. Forry ultimately proved he, like friend H.G. Wells and longtime buddy Isaac Asimov, they were simply ahead of their time. In what was to become a defining moment, Forry not only attended the first World's S/F convention in 1939, in New York he arrived in a homemade 'futuristicostume' that set the stage for countless costume contests and participants to come. Forry found to his surprise, and to everyone else's, he was the only person that dressed up. When WWII drove home the real life horror of war, S/F took a back seat. Forry enlisted and worked as a wartime correspondent for the Fort McArthur bulletin. After a 'three year, 4 month, 29 days" stint in the army during WWII, he went on to become a literary agent to over 200 writers including Asimov, Rod Serling, A. E. Von Vogt and an early science fiction writer known as L. Ron Hubbard. In earlier days of S/F, writers didn't have agents as much as they had connections. Ackerman even kept copies of stories he rejected. Stephen King was astounded when Forry showed up at a King book signing holding a manuscript King had written and submitted when he was only 11.

Since Forry loved a good story as much as the next agent, it is fun to look back and hear how he said the now-famous term of Sci-Fi was coined. It's 1954 and Ackerman was driving down the street with his wife when he looked in the rear-view mirror. He stuck out his tongue, and there, tattooed on the end of it, was the term Sci-Fi. His wife's advice? "Forget it, Forry, it will *never* catch on." Growing older no doubt healed the markings, but thank God it never changed his sense of humor.

Forry's style, informal and friendly, was to serve him in good stead in the years ahead. He was to go on and became a shooting star in the S/F galaxy. Ackerman received S/F's biggest honor in 1953 when he became recipient of the first Hugo Award, for being such a prominent spokesman. Ackerman then kicked up the interest another level when he introduced the ground-breaking genre specific magazine, Famous Monsters of Filmland. It was partially put together by Ackerman's monsterous collection of over 35,000 stills. At the time, Sci-Fi was actually something parents encouraged their children to stay away from because of all the sexy and lurid artwork which artists would decorate the covers to attract buyers. Skeptics

initially called it Forrest's folly, but the first issue went on to sell a startling 200,000 copies. The ten year old in all of us had spoken. At last, organization had arrived for all the unknown collectors. As he would later recall on his MySpace account, "I founded and edited Famous Monsters of Filmland that brought Halloween to kids around the World every month for almost 200 issues and almost 30 years." Ackerman's sense of humor made sure it was going to be great fun as well as entertaining. FMF succeeded because of Ackerman's swift mind, which could take a horror saying and turn it inside out to make a joke or a terrible pun out of it. "Heard about the café on the moon? Good food, but no atmosphere!" The first generation of fanzine geekdom were taken on a tour of monsterdom every issue, with special emphasis on the little guy, the behind the scene worker such as makeup or special effects. Readers were encouraged to not only write, but to send in their own pictures as well. Or call which they could because Uncle Forry's phone number, 213-Moonfan, was also in the magazine. The magazine became the secret hiding spot every enthusiast could hide out once a month. It was, as film director Joe Dante would put it, 'the monster clubhouse.' Filmland fans must have celebrated like vampires at a blood bank.

Every movement needs a charismatic leader to show the fans the way, and 4E was born for the part. He went from being the ultimate collector to the grown up professional with the soul of a nine year old, driver of a literary hearse that finally stopped and delivered their own ghoulish brand of Shakespeare. It sent a ripple thru out a loosely banded community there is now a face that can guide the grass roots movement. Best of all, you could take solace in the fact there wasn't just yourself, but literally millions like you across the nation, if not the world. For all of fandom that ever felt neglected or an 'outie' on the fringe of society, they now had someone to look up to. Legitimacy for all things that go bump in the night had been born, and became a howling success from the beginning. Fans finally found a sense of belonging, a type of identity, and an occupation to get into that was refreshingly different. As he would recall later, "I regard myself as a sci-fi sponge that should be squeezed for information and anecdotes as long as I'm here. So while I'm still around, squeeze me."

Like readers of comics, who always wished their parents were real life super heroes, their adopted father had finally arrived. His car had license plates that said 'SCI FI', and his cavernous house on Glendower drive in 'Hollyweird, Karloffornia' was a fan boy's dream come to life. In an 18 room combination house and museum, complete with secret passageways and a basement filled to the spider-webbing with sacred artifacts of S/F books, masks, paintings, models, hardback, paperbacks, and autographed photos, it was like entering a modern day haunted tomb, and finding different types of treasure from Hollywood's private closets hung up or displayed. The past came alive from the moment you entered, and all the future you saw seemed moments, not light years away. Not only did he house the world's largest private collection of S/F artifacts, on weekends it was an open museum to a curious and grateful public. Once inside, you could touch many of the souvenirs of Hollywood's past. It could

be said Forry in no small amount helped to popularize collecting. He spoke the fankid language and more; he was also fluent in Esperanto, *La Internacia Lingvo*, a constructed language developed by L.L. Zamenhof in the late 1870's in hopes of further uniting people separated by a language barrier. Forry and his beloved German wife Wendy Wahrman, who passed in 1990, at one time estimated they admitted over 50,000 weekend guests to see the Promised Land of Science Fiction and its reigning minister. Since Forry would go out of his way to secure new pieces for *the collection*, as it was called, fans tended to think of it as living and breathing, growing into a new shape before their very eyes. *It's alive, it's alive!* He was the cosmic collector feeding his own personal monster, one whose appetite threatened to never stop expanding, holding a fascination to those who entered on weekends. If ever a fan boy thought someday they'd pass away and go to Heaven, they could be sure it would look a lot like the Ackermansion.

When the fifties and sixties passed into nostalgia, the classic monsters were forgotten and movies changed to embrace the three B's: blood, bimbos, and 'bots. Competition from other magazines became the wolf bane that robbed the subscription rolls at FMF. That double punch plus changes in the horror genre that forgot the original classic monsters left FMF with a situation that pleased neither fan nor publisher. When the magazine folded in 1982, Forry continued as an actor, writer, publisher, literary agent, and Sci-Fi's unofficial host. His role became that of the elder statesman at hundreds of conventions, the equivalent of the first S/F rock star. 4SJ was unique in an occupation filled with unique people, and he kept the excitement going even up to the time of his death of old age in 2008. If Forry J was alive today, he'd be in a reality show on cable. It would probably be called the Real World of Sci-Fi, hosted by Dr. Ackula. Even at the end, he left us a message; his tombstone read simply, 'Sci-Fi Was My High'.

As Ackerman was fond of stating in later years, Sci-Fi enabled him to meet people from all famous walks of life. S/F gave him an opportunity to work at jobs he may have never come in contact with. It took him places he could never go, from the center of the earth to the end of the galaxy. That's quite an accomplishment for a nine year old.

"Reality is that which, when you stop believing in it, doesn't go away."
Philip K. Dick (1928-1982)

If the writers from previous ages could be described as cultured and educated gentlemen trying to get across an important social idea, then Philip Kindred Dick could best be described as the restless soul who spent a tormented lifetime wrestling with those ideas and trying to make them explain his reason

and purpose for existence. Asking 'what is reality' became the focal point of his writings as well as his muddled everyday survival. A self-described 'flipped-out freak', Dick sold his first story in 1951, then followed it up with his first book in 1955. But he and then-wife Kleo Apostolides lived an impoverished life in the fifties waiting for his material to gain public notice. It was neatly summed up by Dick when he deadpanned, "We couldn't even pay the late fees on a library book." As of today's date, films made on Dicks stories have made over one billion dollars.

Titles of his most popular works flow with imaginative names of 'Do Androids Dream of Electric Sheep?', 'Flow My Tears, the Policeman Said', and 'The Three Stigmata of Palmer Eldritch.' His works frequently questioned the true nature of the world. Reality was merely a shifting sands, one that could and will change at any minute, leaving the protagonist and the reader in an altered state of consciousness, possibly a drug induced world, or even another universe, making you wonder which was real and which was better. His ideas made you look in several new directions at the same time and experience the heady rush of discovering nothing you believe lasts even a short time, and the only constant is change. It was like being hit with a tsunami of information, all of it contradictory to what you believed was correct in your everyday existence. When you were finished reading the story, it was like stepping out of a steam bath, but one in which your mind went thru the cleansing process. It was a workout for the intellect, one that exercised our beliefs with plenty of doubt, yet invigorated the psyche with the ideas that were planted. The stories he wrote began to be every bit as trippy as some of the visions he experienced after a 1974 wisdom tooth extraction. The visions became more frequent and longer in duration, to the point where Dick thought himself to live a double life, one as himself, the other as a persecuted ichthys in the time of Christ. These bifurcated beliefs became the basis for the Valis (Vast Active Living Intelligence System) trilogy.

Like all great authors, Dick's books proved to define the culture we live in, now and will continue to do so in the future. By using themes of blurred reality, looking glass religion, an absorption with war, recurring mental illness, unpredictable drug use, and two faced governments where the secret rich rule, he produced tales with an unrelenting undercurrent of paranoia about the police enforcing an ever-tightening net over the minutia of the common man, where the future is not only bleak, it's not even guaranteed.

Dick's Hugo and Nebula award winning prose was fast paced and gripping entertainment that would bust out of the starters gate like a thoroughbred and never slow down till you reached the finish line. His ideas were like the visionaries before him, but with a darker tone, one that forced you to confront your own dreams about the future and ask if they really weren't nightmares in disguise. It was not unlike being on a roller coaster with dangerous curves and a safe port to finally pull into, knowing it was all over. But when you look behind you, it's ready to start up all over again. You could win momentarily, but the shadow rulers were always ready to come back. In Dick's stories, victory

was short lived and change seemed to be a lifetime away. If life were a card game, then it was a cinch the aces were taken out of the deck and the jokers were going to show up sooner or later.

Dick was a man who would obsessively write in the hope he would be able to understand the baffling curves in his short 53 year life, especially the ones that kept him from ever clearly seeing what his existence was based on and its purpose. By incessantly writing and using this as a catharsis it wound up in an 8000 page amphetamine-fueled catharsis he titled Exegesis, all in an attempt to comprehend the shifting realities that would define his life. But he never reached the security of a port, wrestling with his fate and pondering his own state of mind and problems with schizophrenia and paranoia up to February 17, 1982, when he was found unconscious in his home in Santa Ana, California of a stroke. After being taken to the hospital, he suffered another one, and on March 2 his family gave consent to have him taken off support. He died shortly thereafter.

Dick's crystal ball was his typewriter, and he used it to rail against what he saw as the inevitable erosion of the individual's right against a shadow government, located in between the present and the near future. It was in plain sight yet invisible, unable to grasp yet powerful enough to crush an entire class of people, all controlling but unable to stamp out a single persons dream of freedom and life. His stories spoke out against a continued government ruling class and religion, with us, the common man, as the seeker for truth, the traveler searching for a meaning to the undefined forces that rage against them, struggling to get a grip against the organized chaos that never permits the individual to get a firm footing on their life and the future that will almost surely control them.

It was a fight against becoming a flesh and blood robot, at the cost of losing everything, even the society the individual lived in. Dick needn't have worried; that same society was the one that published his stories, his books, his ideas, and his movies that a grateful free populace would see and absorb. As long as those ideals are here, and men like Verne, Wells, Gurning, Burroughs, Ackerman, and Dick are here to pass the lamp of knowledge, then androids will always be able to dream of electronic sheep.

Here we have one Frenchman, one Englishman, one Luxembourg, two from Chicago Illinois, one from Los Angeles, California. Every one of these came from differing backgrounds of money, culture, beliefs, and environment. They all shared the common goal, however, of teaching a still-young world about better ways to live and the consequences if we didn't learn from the past and our experiences. Science Fiction wasn't created with one common background, or even creators speaking the same language, but it was forged and welded with a common ambition to deliver one thing: the future.

In 2026, Science Fiction will celebrate its one hundredth anniversary. Sci-Fi, like education, had its three R's; robots, rocket ships and ray guns. With the blast off of computers and the effect this had on bringing previously unmade works to the silver screen, S/F made a quantum leap forward towards making stories into the next level of entertainment, and a step closer towards making the inventions real. A fourth R could be added to both education and Sci-Fi's list; reboot. Because computers and Ohm's law will remain the driving force for any type of success in the S/F movie field, computer studies will become a standard to be mastered by children. It becomes easy to predict the line between special effects and real life will become blurred to such an extent that it will become impossible to tell even by experts if a scene is real or generated. More than worlds will be created; it will become universes, with stories of lands light years away and heroes of every pedigree created for the entertainment that have always embraced the dreams of tomorrow. When it does happen, and that day is rapidly approaching, we'll have reached another plateau in the field in both S/F and entertainment. Reality will have become merged with dreams, and it will be *Dreality*. Maybe even more fantastic inventions that we couldn't imagine now will become true, such as a digital VCR that could record our dreams. Who could resist? When that day arrives, the goal of S/F will have gone full circle, and what started out as a dream will have turned wishes into fulfillment. That is what the meaning of the original S/F was; to open our eyes to see the unlimited potential that our society could make itself become, and the wonderful inventions that could come about as a result of that. What the meaning of the original S/F was; to open our eyes to see the unlimited potential that our society could make itself become, and the wonderful inventions that could come about as a result of that. Perhaps the name of Science Fiction will be renamed, and it will be known as Science Faction, a combination of fact and fiction. What started out as dreams woven on paper has become true to life, and once more an idea will have proven to be worth more than guns in moving a world closer to an ideal society. The magazines and comic books were all filled with variations of finding the nirvanas of civilization out in the stars, but it will be found here on Earth, created by those people who not only dared to dream, but put the power of their convictions behind it and lived that way. They became what they wrote about, and made life a little bit easier for millions of people to come. If this is what it turns out to be when people have the luxury to dream, then maybe a fifth R, Re-imagine, will find itself on the list. We certainly couldn't ask for anything less.

*** Philip Marsh is a graduate of CSU Fullerton and has a Bachelor's in Sociology. He spent three years as a student, one year finding his parking space. His house is decorated in early American confusion. His favorite pasttime is spending money. He welcomes all criticisms, comments, and compliments on his work at philipmarsh@aol.com. ***

From the Earth to the Moon – Jules Verne

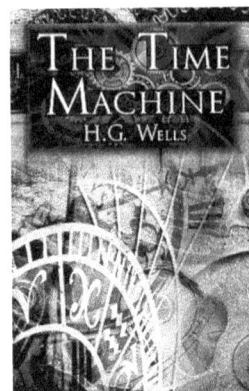

The Time Machine – H.G. Wells

Ralph 124C41+ - Hugo Gernsback

Lost on Venus - Edgar Rice Burroughs

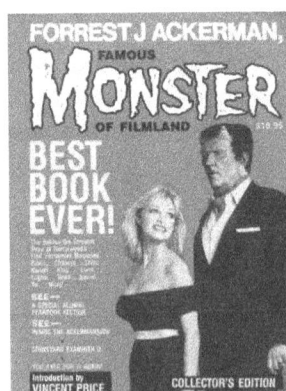

Famous Monsters of Filmland – Forrest J. Ackerman

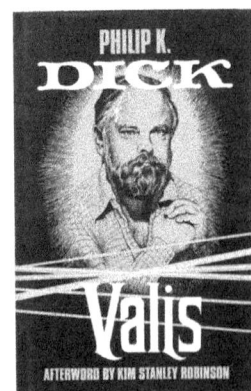

Valis - Philip K. Dick

Genuine Richard Nixon Signed Photo and Letter

Dated January 19, 1961, this letter is show as coming from the "Official of the Vice President" on its masthead. Content includes talking about the 1960 Presidential campaign. Both the letter and photo are signed. Envelope has water stain on left 1/3 side.

Asking $1,000 plus shipping and handling.

Send all inquiries to philipmarsh@aol.com. All questions and e-mail will be answered.

ART TATUM   GALE INC.
                                                  58 West 48th Street
                                                  New York 19, N.Y.

Tantalizing Tatum: What was Art's Mark?

By Larry Rafferty

If you check the lists of the most gifted jazz pianists of the 20th Century, Art Tatum's name often tops the list. When I first began collecting jazz autographs seriously in the early 1980s, I put together a want list of anout fifteen names. This was my short list of the rarest and most desirable autographs. One of the names on it was Art Tatum. Many years went by and I never saw or heard of a Tatum autograph. Then, in 1990 I received a dealer's sale list that had an album page signed by Art Tatum!

I immediately phone in my order, and waited anxiously. However, when it arrived, I felt uneasy. The autograph didn't look "right." Art Tatum was, of course, legally blind. He was totally blind in one eye, and had just enough vision in the other to avoid bumping into large objects. People with little or no vision *can* learn to write, but not with the small, neat even flow of this example. Shortly after I obtained this piece, I attended a convention of jazz record collectors. I had the occasion to meet Arnold Laubich, who had written the discography of Tatum. He told me that he did not believe that Tatum could

write. While he was researching his book, Arnold had access to Tatum's estate papers. In them he found nothing written in Tatum's hand. On the strength of this I returned the autograph to the dealer for a refund.

A year or so later I told this story to a customer of mine. He responded by sending me a Xerox copy of a photo in the Time-Life *Giants of Jazz* series that purports to show Tatum 'signing' autographs. This seemed to kick the door back open; maybe he could write.

In 1993 I received a catalog from a prominent New York auction house. It contained an 8x10 signed photograph of (you're way ahead of me)...Art Tatum. I called the auctioneer and asked if he could provide me with provenance for this item. His reply was the non-responsive, "I have no reason to doubt it." I declined to bid. The lot sold for $660. The next year another east coast dealer offered a Tatum signature. This one looked like it could have been written with the same hand as the photo above. Doubt about Mr. Laubich's hypothesis began to creep back in.

In September of 1995 I attended a classic cinema convention at the Hollywood Roosevelt Hotel. A movie memorabilia dealer there who knew I collected jazz autographs offered me a number of royalty checks he'd picked up from a music publishing firm that had been signed by jazz musicians. The checks were all typed on the front and endorsed on the back by their recipients. As I was going through them, I came to a check made out to "Art Tatum." You can imagine my emotions as I turned the check over. On the back of the check was an "X" that was attested to by two witnesses. This evidence seems virtually conclusive as to the question of whether Art Tatum could write or not.

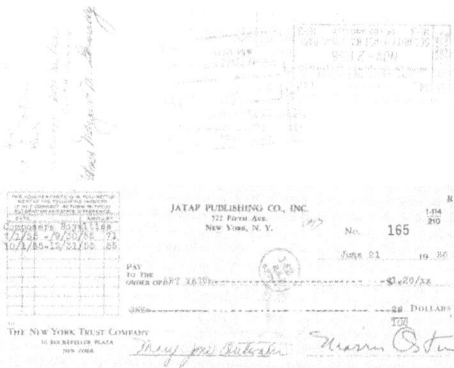

Art Tatum check signed with an "X"

After sharing this momentous find with a few friends, one of them mentioned that James Lester's book *Too Marvelous for Words* had something in it about Tatum using a rubber stamp. I wrote to Mr. Lester and he was generous enough to call me and share what information he had. His opinion paralleled Mr. Laubich's. He had seen Tatum's passport application and one contract, both signed with "X"s. He had neither seen nor heard of any holograph material by Tatum in researching his biography.

A few weeks later I picked up my final exhibit. A gentleman contacted me who said he had attended a New York City club date in 1952, and after the first set approached Art for an autograph. Tatum pulled a rubber stamp and pad from his pocket and gave him his "autograph." This, of course, not only confirms Lester, it answers the question raised by the Time-Life photo.

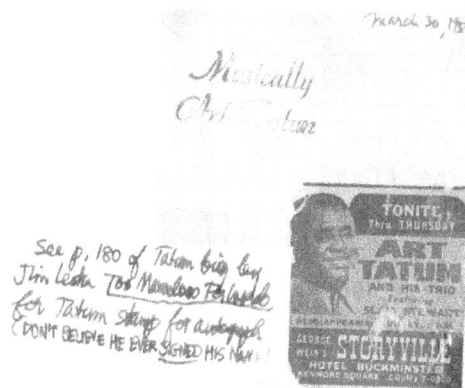

Art Tatum "autograph" rubber stamp

While the evidence is still scant, I feel that it strongly suggests that the purported autographs of Art Tatum are not genuine (other than an "X" or Tatum's stamp, of course). Certainly, the burden of proof weighs heavily on those claiming to own valid signatures.

Over the years I've often been asked to authenticate signatures. This can be tricky, especially if the signature is rare. It can take years of research to feel confident that a signature is genuine. In the end it comes down to evidence, provenance, and exemplars. Without those, authentication is impossible. I've been lucky to get many signatures either in person or from individuals who got them in person, and build a file of exemplars. In Art's case, I stand by his "X"!

Dr. Sandor Tarics: The World's Oldest Living Olympic Champion

By Dorina Marian

Dr. Sandor Tarics, the world's oldest living Olympic champion turned 100 years old on September 23, 2013. Tarics was a member of the Gold Medal-winning Hungarian water polo team in 1936. I have the chance to conduct a telephone interview with him, since he lives in California in the United States. He sent me several photos. When signing, he uses both of his first names: Alexander in English and Sandor in Hungarian.

D.M.: *You were born in Obuda, Budapest in 1913. What kind of memories do you have about your childhood?*

S.T.: "My father was a carpenter and my mother was a dressmaker. I studied hard since my parents were telling me the only way to get a better life is to study and to get more knowledge than others, because the competition is hard, mainly among boys. I attended the Technical University in Budapest and I got my degree in 1936, the same year of the Berlin Olympic Games. Later I did more scientific work and received my doctor degree in 1943."

D.M.: *When and how did you get involved in water polo? Did you know Bela Komjadi, the pioneer in Hungarian water sports?*

S.T.: "In the secondary grammar school I was a member of our school water polo team. Bela Komjadi once saw me in the water playing and invited me to the trainings of a special junior team selected to prepare young athletes for future Olympics. So I went and started to take water polo seriously. In summer we had water trainings. In winter we practiced boxing, because there were no indoor pools. Komjadi taught us that water polo was a rough game. You should not be afraid of getting hurt, but you should not be the first one to hit. The aim is winning the match, not fighting. Anyway, sometimes the watned turned to be pinkish."

D.M.: *You participated at the Berlin Olympic Games in 1936 as a member of the Hungarian Water Polo team. Could you feel the political atmosphere?*

S.T.: "Hitler opened and closed the 1936 Berlin Olympic Games. When I arrived at the Olympics, it was like a German military camp. There were uniformed soldiers and swastikas everywhere. Our team pushed the German water polo team into second place and won the Gold Medal. Hitler was so disappointed he did not even congratulate the Hungarian water polo team."

Swimming Stadium - Berlin Olympics, 1936

D.M.: *Do you remember any curious event?*

S.T.: "We were watching the water polo game when I heard the noises of cameras taking photos. Then it turned out that a woman climbed over the fences and hugged Hitler. This Brazilian woman made a bet with her friends that she would do it. Of course, when she hugged Hitler the soldiers were on her. But she could have even killed Hitler if she had anything in her hand. The next day I read in the paper that 30 German bodyguards were dismissed."

D.M.: *It was highly difficult for Jewish sportsmen to get into the German Olympic Team. Foreign countries were worried about organizing the Olympic Games in a country where anit-semitism was so obvious, so Hitler allowed some "half-Jewish" sportsmen and women to participate in the German team?*

S.T.: "Yes, for example in Women's Fencing, the silver medalist was Helene Mayer, a half-Jewish lady from Germany. The gold medalist was Ilona Elek from Hungary. Origin was not an issue in other countries' Olympic teams. From Hungary, several Jewish sportsmen and women participated in the Berlin Olympic Games. Hungary won 10 gold medals, five of them won by Jewish people. The eight individual and two team gold medals made Hungary a sport empire."

GOLD MEDAL COUNT

German Empire – 33
United States – 24
Hungary – 10
Italy – 8
Finland – 7
France – 7
Sweden – 6
Japan – 6
The Netherlands – 6
Great Britain – 4
Austria – 4
Czechoslovakia – 3

Adolf Hitler Watching the 1936 Games

D.M.: *I could not find any high quality photo about the Hungarian water polo team in the Berlin Olympics. Could you send me one?*

S.T.: "Unfortunately not. During World War II, our house was in the Buda side of the city, situated in the frontline. First it was bombed by the Germans, the rest was destroyed by the Russians. We lost everything. After the fights I went there and was picking the debris. That is how I found my gold medal of 1936. But all photos and documents were burnt. There is no photo remained at all with all the 11 members of our teams. On the photo I signed for you two players are missing. I hope you like all of the six photos I signed for you."

Dr Alexander – Sándor – Tarics
olympic champion
1936

D.M.: *Of course. That you indeed. I am sure your signed photos will have a great success among the autograph collectors. By the way, what made you leave Hungary and move to the United States in 1948?*

S.T.: Politicial turnover happened in Hungary and many of my Jewish friends were loaded onto trains headed for Auschwitz. Russians invaded Hungary and occupied Budapest on February 13, 1945. Later I was investgated by communist committees. They took away my voting rights. If you have no voting rights, then you're nobody. I had my engineering degree and I got a teaching fellowship and a visa. First I went to teach at a university in Indiana. I was also looking for other opportunities."

1936 Hungarian Olympic Water Polo Team

D.M.: *Did you play water polo or any other sport in the U.S.A.?*

S.T.: "With five or six friends of mine we decided to play tennis, so we built a tennis club in 1950. Today 250 families are the members of this club. There is a swimming pool, seven tennis courts and a gym. I am the only living founder of the club. The other members are proud of me because they know that I am an Olympic champion. Of course, I was swimming regularly and nowadays I take long walks to keep me fit."

D.M.: *Did you work as an engineer?*

S.T.: "I had a long, successful career designing buildings for earthquake safety. I became the CEO of a company and we designed more than 500 schools, universities, hospitals, five subway stations in San Francisco, and special purpose military buildings. I was 75 when I sold my company and I continued my work in a smaller one specializing in earthquake safety for another 10 years. After that I retired."

D.M.: *When was the first time you visited Hungary?*

S.T.: "In 1964. I was already a U.S. citizen. 16 years had gone by since I left my country. There was a very large amount of hard communism in Hungary. The Hungarian Swimming Association, including my old coach, was waiting for me at the railroad station. I knew all of them. I even got a bouquet of roses in my room at Hotel Gellert and everybody was very kind to me. I really enjoyed myself."

D.M.: *You had your 99th birthday in September, 2012. Your intellectual and physical freshness is admirable. How do you spend a day?*

S.T.: "My wife and I get up in the morning. First I read the newspaper. If I am not in the "Obituary" column, I go on with my work. I still deal with mathematics. I am very bad at languages. It took years to learn proper English. In contrast, I have a natural talent for math."

D.M.: *You were at the London Olympic Games as a guest of honor of the Hungarian Olympic Committee. What was that like?*

S.T.: "I met the athletes of other nations as well, but I rooted only for the Hungarians. I hope I can make it to 103 to root for the Hungarian water polo team in the 2016 Olympics in Rio de Janeiro."

D.M.: *You speak impeccable Hungarian. I cannot notice that you*

have been living in the U.S.A. since 1948. Why is that so?

S.T.: "My wife Elisabeth and I always speak Hungarian at home."

1936 Hungarian Water Polo Team

Signed photo sent to Dorina Marian

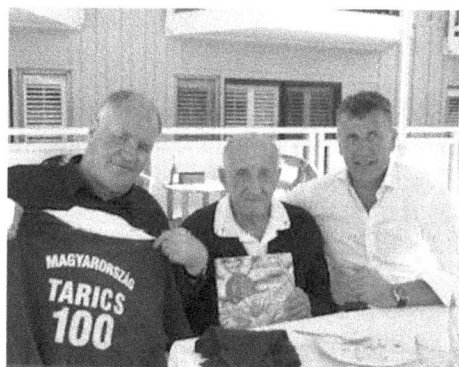
100th Birthday celebration with the Hungarian Olympic Committee Officials

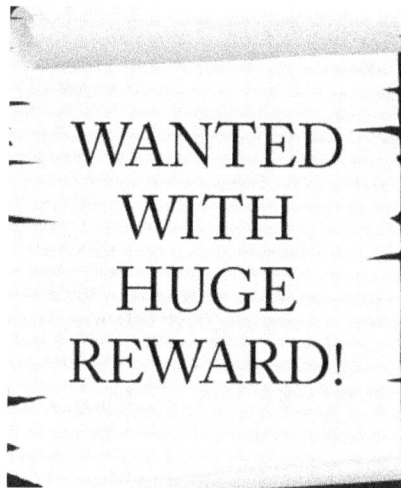

The Autograph Hobby's First Wanted Poster?

By Stephen Koschal

I was curious if anyone in the hobby of collecting autographs or something associated with the hobby ever produced a "Wanted Poster." Club journals from time to time would run a paid advertisement from a collector for a signature that they wanted for their collection. However, that's as close as I could find until June, 2004, when I received a wonderful catalog from Leland's Sports Auctions. To my surprise, after thumbing through the catalog, the next to last page was a full page devoted to offering a "$1 Million Dollar Reward."

The reward wass for the home run baseball hit by Bobby Thomson off pitcher Ralph Branca on October 3, 1951.

That hit is known as "The Shot Heard Round the World." Many baseball fans and sports historians refer to that hit as the "greatest moment in baseball history." That hit captured the hearts of baseball fans worldwide and broke the hearts of fans of the Brooklyn Dodgers. That hit won the pennant for the New York Giants.

Many still recall broadcaster Russ Hodges screaming on the microphone: "The Giants win the pennant! The Giants win the pennant! The Giants win the pennant!" The fans went crazy as Bobby Thomson hit the ball into the lower deck of the left field stands.

This remarkable feat happened over 60 years ago and that treasured baseball has not been seen since.

According to Josh Evans of Leland's, "The Thomson home run is often considered the greatest single moment in baseball history; the culmination of a miracle comeback by the New York Giants to take a 4-2 deficit in the last of the ninth and turn it into a 5-4 victory over arch-rival Brooklyn."

Photographic evidence of the home run ball reaching the stands in the Polo Grounds exists. A man appears to have caught the ball.

Leland's Reward Poster states: "To anyone who can come forth with the baseball, and with sufficient evidence to show that the man in the picture has the ball, or that there is a trail of evidence that shows the existence of the ball today, Leland's.com is offering a $1 million dollar reward. Leland's will auction the ball and guarantee $1 million to the owner, making up the difference in the auction if need be. It might go for more!"

The illustration below is the $1 million dollar reward.

$1 MILLION DOLLAR REWARD

Since I never saw a Reward Poster issued about a collectible, I decided to send my poster to Bobby Thomson for his autograph. He was kind enough to return it inscribed to me and dating the poster "Oct. 3, 1951." Days later, I sent the same poster to the Dodger pitcher Ralph Branca for his autograph. Within a week, my item was returned inscribed and signed. In my mind, to complete the poster with autographs, it would be necessary for me to get the autograph of the person offering the $1 million reward. I met Josh Evans at one of the National Sports Card shows and asked him to sign my poster. To my surprise he wrote, "To Steve – not the right photo but the offer is still good."

For all I know, this signed poster may be unique. When I spoke to Bobby Thomson a few years later he didn't recall signing another. That's when I had him sign one more.

Not surprisingly, people have come forward producing a Warren Giles National League ball, trying to collect the reward. However, according to a follow up with Josh Evans, one 65-year-old individual did produce what he claimed to be the home run ball from the famous game. From the discussion, Evans believed the ball did come from the famous game but it could not be verified with certainty that it was the home run ball hit by Thomson because no irrefutable evidence could be produced. Therefore, the ball could not properly be authenticated.

Now that Bobby Thomson has passed on, there's no chance of more of these types of unusual collectibles to be signed… or is there? Keep reading Autograph Quarterly for an amazing related story.

October 4, 1951 Daily News Cover
Photo Courtesy of the New York Daily News

Who Was Paul McCullough?

By Todd Mueller
(with biographical information courtesy of Wikipedia)

Born on March 27, 1883, Paul McCullough was an American actor and comedian who appeared in circuses and vaudeville revues before making it in mainstream stardom with partner Bobby Clark. Most known for the comedy team Clark and McCullough, Paul and Bobby met at a local Y.M.C.A. when they were children.

Their childhood friendship grew into an adult partnership, and the pair made several appearances in circuses around the country and many vaudeville revues before getting their big break in the 1922 Irving Berlin Broadway show *Music Box Revue*.

Their later Broadway hit The Ramblers was filmed in 1930 as The Cuckoos, a vehicle for Wheeler and Woolsey. Clark and McCullough went to Hollywood in 1928 and starred in 35 short films produced over a seven-year period.

In their act, Clark was the dominant, motor-mouthed comedian while Paul McCullough was the quieter straight man. In many of their films, McCullough's input was severely limited to a supporting role as Clark

generated the bulk of the humor. Their occupations in the films usually dictated what Clark's character was: when photographers, such as in Alibi Bye Bye, Clark was named "Flash"; when chefs, Clark was "Cook"; when lawyers, Clark was "Blackstone", etc…

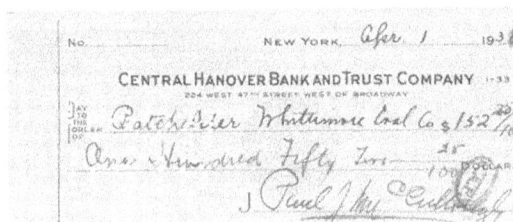

Bank check courtesy of Todd Mueller Autographs

Paul McCullough was always named "Blodgett" regardless of the role. The Clark and McCullough film series ended in 1935. Having completed their last short for R.K.O., McCullough and Clark went on tour in a version of George White's Scandals. The frenetic pace of touring emotionally discombobulated McCullough and, suffering from nervous exhaustion, he entered a sanitarium in Medford, Massachusetts. In March, 1936, he was released. As he was driving home with a friend, he decided to have a shave. They stopped at a local barber shop where McCullough struck up a friendly conversation with the barber. Without warning, as the barber's back was turned, McCullough grabbed a straight razor and slashed his own throat and wrists. In critical condition, he was taken to a nearby hospital where he died several days later.

Clark, upon learning of his partner's death, publicly stated; "I think it was just something Paul couldn't help. Something that had been with him all the time and he didn't even know it."

Clark, who was emotionally devastated by the loss of his old friend, made only one film appearance as a solo performer, in The Goldwyn Follies in 1938 and died in 1960.

The great comedy team of Clark and McCullough are little known in the 21st century, despite their great popularity in the first half of the 20th century. One of the reasons likely is the fact that their short films were not packaged and sold to television in the 1950s, unless The Three Stooges and Laurel and Hardy, who then went on to entertain new generations of fans. Bobby Clark wrote much of the dialogue, and it was very risque and considered borderline in the more liberal 1930s.

Clark and McCullough shorts were geared towards adults, and thus would have been inappropriate on television in the 1950s, as the comedy shorts of The Three Stooges and Laurel and Hardy were programmed for children. The short films of the equally famous in the 1930s and now almost forgotten comedy team of Wheeler and Woolsey were never released to commerical television either, as they were considered to be too vulgar.

Clark and McCullough as clowns

Kicking the Crown Around

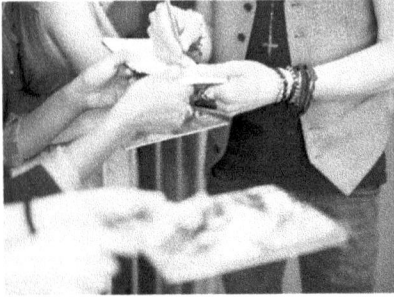

Autograph Runners: Meet the People Behind the Scenes

As a first in autograph magazines, we want to highlight interesting tips, stories and the like from those intrepid souls the industry calls runners. They are the men and women who wait hours on end to get a tough star to sign a photograph, card, guitar, or baseball for them in person most of whom sell them to dealers. Here are some of their current stories in their own words.

Harry Styles of *One Direction* is often out and about with new girlfriend Kendall Jenner. They were just sighted at the L.A. restaurant Craigs where he did sign for fans, but he signs CDs and photographs mostly. When he thinks the item is valuable, such as a guitar pick guard, he will sign his name in block letters supposedly hurting its value. Not a real graph you know…

Harry Styles signing in London
Photo by Dave Hogan

One Direction in L.A. almost always stays at the W Resort in Westwood and security with all the screaming girls is too tight for autograph runners, that is except the smart ones who book rooms there and say the boys will happily sign for them at the pool, in hallways, eating, and even pick up items from the front desk, sign and return them!

James Earl Jones
Photo by Peter Kramer

James Earl Jones was spotted in New York recently. After attending a play's performance, he told the runner if they left his driver the material and address he would sign and return them, but after the play and at over the age of 80, he said he wasn't going to stand the time it would take to sign. True to his word, the items were returned authentically signed a few days later.

Cybill Shepherd once told fans the same story but without the being over 80 part. Those items came back secretarily signed though many with previously signed authentic Bruce Willis signatures from her *Moonlighting* days on them. Thanks for nothing Cybill. She should win our Oinker Award for that!

Cybill Shepherd in *Moonlighting*
Photo courtesy of ABC

Alan Alda is still a terrible signer, purposely going out of his way to try and be ruder than Jerry Lewis.

Alan Alda
Photo courtesy of NBC

Need Schwarzenegger? He frequents Café Roma and has been working out at the same gym in Santa Monica for years. Go check it out!

Arnold Schwarzenegger
Photo by Jason Laveris

Diana Ross said on *Oprah* she had three pet peeves (only three Diana?).

The first is being called Diana instead of Miss Ross. The second is taking pictures with fans. Most of us know that this won't happen, and number three is signing autographs!

Diana Ross
Photo by Theo Wargo

eBay's hottest signed photographs are lately under the Adults section as more and more celebrities sign blank sheets of photo paper and then the dealers or runners print nudes on the signed area. That would be clever, but they don't care if the nudes are even real or not, and these fake signed nudes are selling for big bucks on eBay. Shame on the runner/dealer who does this, and shame on eBay for allowing it.

And finally, Lady Gaga signed an index card for super collector and dealer Lenora at LAX recently. Gaga does love all her little monsters!

Lady Gaga
Photo by Fred Duval

What's Hot? What's Not?

In autographs, once a person has passed away the autograph values ultimately rise. This is a simple case of supply and demand.

Some celebrities live long lives and sign a lot during their lifetime, so the uptick in value can usually only be seen for a three to six month period right after they pass away when collectors jump into the market to secure a piece for their collection.

Some celebrities die unexpectedly younger or didn't sign many pieces before dying, as in the case of Marlon Brando who, while he lived a long time, never signed much during his life. So his value rose steadily after his death.

Entertainment may not be your bag, but these principles still apply. Take the signers of the Declaration of Independence. Is it any wonder the two that sell for seven figures now are Thomas Lynch and Button Gwinnett? Both died in their 20s leaving a rare cache of signatures to collect from coupled now with it being over 200 years since they signed them. Most of their signatures have already been placed in various institutions.

What's Hot and What's Not also applies to generational collecting, which is why Star Wars is still hot and Harry Potter will heat up again in about ten years as those collectors who grew up on those films start their collections. Some of the things that were previously hot in the past thirty years

Just as I write this, Paul Walker died suddenly in a car crash and while he did sign readily for fans, he wasn't plentiful and as the star of one of the most successful movie series in film history (the Fast and Furious film franchise), his price jumped overnight from $40-$50 on a signed image to well over $400, and in some cases $600-$700! While those prices will settle down, he will still be collected from and for those films at a premium of his pre-deceased price.

that I have been a dealer are decidedly not now.

Academy award collecting has cooled considerably whereas there were many collectors ten years ago still collecting examples of every Best Actor or Best Actress, etc. winner. Now they seem scarce as collectors.

Worldwide famous stars are still hot. In fact, The Beatles, Marilyn Monroe, and

James Dean still shows no sign of slowing in popularity and therefore keep going up in price.

The ones about the enter that same category, which I think you will see a lot of upward movement on price soon would be The Rolling Stones, who every member is still living and touring this year, but for how much longer when the youngest is 73?

For you historical buffs, Amelia Earhart and Thomas Edison are still far too cheap, as is Henry Ford, Alexander Graham Bell, and Harry Houdini.

Presidential set collecting has slowed considerably, while the stand-outs remain hot – Washington, Lincoln, Jefferson, and Kennedy. The rest are at a stand still, at least price wise.

Heath Ledger, a posthumous Academy Award winner for his portrayal of 'The Joker' is another good piece to put away if investment is your game, as well as rarer examples and good content pieces of Michael Jackson, Madonna, Bruce Springsteen, and Bob Dylan in the music department. In the acting department, Paul Newman, Elizabeth Taylor, and Robert Redford are still too cheap.

Knowing when to buy, knowing what's hot and what's not, and having the experts weigh in on the topic in each issue is what this column is all about, and as the editor of the Official Autograph Price Guide, I will also (starting in the next issue) be showing you prices that you can use and count on when looking for pieces for your collection. Until then, what's hot and what's not in your view? Let us know what you think and why!

SOLD!
Auctions in the News

Mantle Contract Fetches Big Bucks for Hurricane Sandy Relief

Mickey Mantle's family sold his 1960 Yankees signed contract recently at auction for $40,000.00. They then donated the entire amount to the Hurricane Sandy relief fund. They did it because the great ball player spent eighteen years of his life living in New Jersey during his Yankees years. New Jersey, of course, was the site hardest hit by the storm. Good job, and hats off to the Mantle family!

Celebrities Donating Their Time

Charity always brings the bigger bucks as evidenced by the person who spent $58,000.00 for a lunch with George Clooney. Another fan spent $130,000.00 for lunch with Sir Paul McCartney. A day hanging out with former President Bill Clinton will set you back $255,000.00.

Oprah Winfrey Hosts the Ultimate Yard Sale!

Oprah Winfrey gave her money to charity after hosting her first "Yard Sale" (as she billed it). The items sold for over $600,000.00!

She said she needed to "de-clutter" her homes with highlights being a 16x20 copy of an Oprah TV Guide cover photo that sold for $3,000.00, a canvas banner showing Oprah in The Color Purple brought $4,100.00, a common nondescript teapot made $1,000.00, and a pair of table lamps (also not very special without shades) sold for over $2,500.00! She gave the money to her own non-profit South African girls school. The auction also included a fleet of seven autographed scooters that by the next day were appearing in eBay auctions by some fearless collectors, or perhaps dealers?

In future issues, we will be covering the autograph auctions as a variety of auction houses supply us with their sales results.

Autograph Exemplars

Julie Andrews

Jim Arness

Anne Bancroft

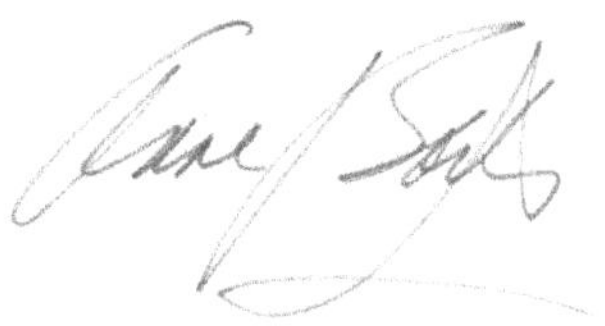

Anne Baxter

Olivia de Havilland

Robert Downey, Jr.

America Ferrera

Flea

Hugh Hefner

Jennifer Jones

Lindsay Lohan

Suzanne Pleshette

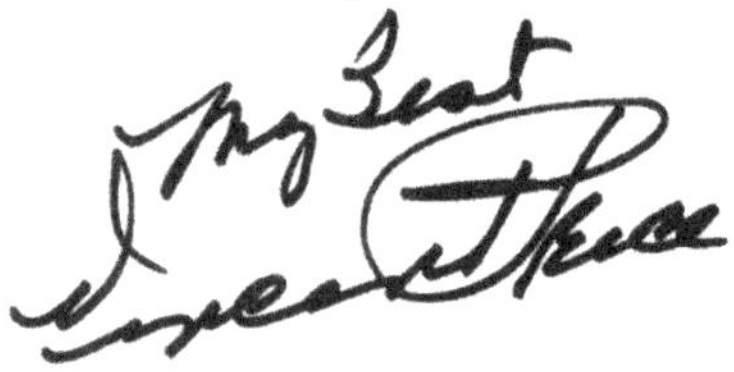

Vincent Price

Denver Pyle

Rob Reiner

Diana Rigg

David Lee Roth

George C. Scott

Chloe Sevigney

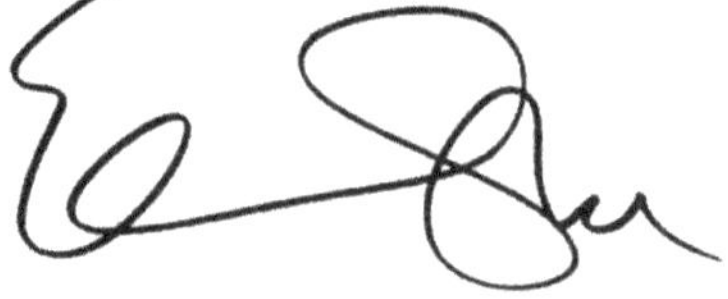

Elizabeth Shue

Can I have your **autograph?**

Now here's a first for an autograph magazine.
Autograph Quarterly will be supplying one absolutely proven
current address to a celebrity in each of our issues. Okay, so
that's not new, but we're not stopping there.

We're giving you a free 8x10 photo to send to the
Celebrity of the Quarter!

Each issue our subscribers will be able to open the back pages
of Autograph Quarterly and be able to send the photo to the
celebrity for signing purposes. The fun part is that you never
know just who that celebrity might be. It could be an up-and-
coming personality. It could be one of your favorite television
or movie stars. It could even be a member of music royalty!

Subscribe today and you'll be adding to your collection soon!